CARLISLE PAPER

THE ROLE OF RELIGION
IN NATIONAL SECURITY POLICY
SINCE SEPTEMBER 11, 2001

Jonathan E. Shaw

February 2011

Comments pertaining to this report are invited and should be forwarded to: Director, Strategic Studies Institute, U.S. Army War College, 122 Forbes Ave, Carlisle, PA 17013-5244.

*****

All Strategic Studies Institute (SSI) publications are available on the SSI homepage for electronic dissemination. Hard copies of this report may also be ordered from our homepage. SSI's homepage address is: *www.StrategicStudiesInstitute.army.mil*.

*****

The Strategic Studies Institute publishes a monthly e-mail newsletter to update the national security community on the research of our analysts, recent and forthcoming publications, and upcoming conferences sponsored by the Institute. Each newsletter also provides a strategic commentary by one of our research analysts. If you are interested in receiving this newsletter, please subscribe on our homepage at *www.StrategicStudiesInstitute.army.mil/newsletter/*.

PREFACE

The U.S. Army War College provides an excellent environment for selected military officers and government civilians to reflect on and use their career experience to explore a wide range of strategic issues. To assure that the research conducted by Army War College students is available to Army and Department of Defense leaders, the Strategic Studies Institute publishes selected papers in its "Carlisle Papers" Series.

ANTULIO J. ECHEVARRIA II
Director of Research
Strategic Studies Institute

ABOUT THE AUTHOR

JONATHAN E. SHAW is a U.S. Army Chaplain (Colonel) currently assigned as Command Chaplain, Combined Arms Center and Fort Leavenworth, Kansas. His service began in 1974 in the U.S. Army Reserve Officer Training Corps, and has included civilian parishes in Guadalajara, Mexico, and Virginia. He has served continuously since 1984 as a U.S. Army Chaplain, serving in military units from battalion to Department of the Army, with deployments to Honduras, Panama, and Iraq. He served as an ethics instructor for U.S. Army officers (1999-2002). Chaplain Shaw has published extensively in professional journals and military publications in the areas of U.S. Army religious support doctrine, world religions, ethics, liturgics, homiletics, exegesis, and systematic theology. He is a founding editor of *Gottesdienst,* and has served as Chairman of the Board, District and Congregational Services of the Lutheran Church-Missouri Synod, his Department of Defense Ecclesiastical Endorsing Agency. Chaplain Shaw holds a BA in Political Science from Wheaton College, IL, a BA in Ethics from Vanderbilt, an M.Div. in Pastoral Theology and an S.T.M. in Systematic Theology from Concordia Theological Seminary, a Diploma from the U.S. Army Command and General Staff College, and an M.S.S. from the U.S. Army War College.

ABSTRACT

The United States has struggled to find a framework to integrate religion into the post-September 11, 2001 (9/11) discussion of national security. Islam has been the central focus, with both the 9/11 terrorists and many of America's partners in overseas contingency operations sharing an Islamic heritage.

The struggle to locate that framework has taken the United States down a number of roads since the turn of the millennium, none of which has been totally satisfactory. President George W. Bush viewed freedom as a universal value, with religious freedom as the preeminent characteristic of free, robust societies. With this assumption, he viewed the post-9/11 conflict with the Taliban and al-Qaeda as a battle over freedom. He believed that repressed Iraqis and Afghans would welcome the U.S. military as liberators bringing greater freedom, to include freedom of religion. President Bush's assumptions were only partially validated. Part of the problem was the dissonance between a Western concept of freedom to choose and worship God over against an Islamic concept to submit to God. Bush's construct of Religion as Freedom did not offer the optimal framework.

Neither has President Barack Obama's Religion as Unity framework solved the problem. President Obama has asserted a universal value regarding religion—that all religions are united by a moral law to care for one's fellowman. Based on this assumption, President Obama has labeled radical Muslim terrorists as false Muslims, and also launched initiatives to honor Islam and resolve mutual misunderstandings through dialog with Muslim states. His efforts have succeeded partially, but radical traditionalist Muslims continue to fight, believing they are the pure practitioners of the faith. Also, President Obama's framework has not accounted for the large numbers of Muslims in Muslim-majority countries who find terrorism sometimes justifiable. An additional framework is needed, one that understands religion as power which is comprehended in grand strategy, and religion as behavior which is addressed in policy.

To begin to derive such a framework, it is helpful to look forward, to project the potential scope of the interplay between religion and national security. An examination of the enduring role of religion in human conflict through the eyes of Alvin Toffler, Francis Fukuyama, Samuel Huntington, and Robert Kaplan proves helpful. Toffler, Fukuyama, Huntington, and Kaplan articulate different visions of the current and future world, with varying views of national security challenges. Each author, however, includes religion as a critical component in any policy that would address those challenges effectively, and highlights Islam within that process.

Current and projected U.S. national security challenges highlight the need to explore Islam's historical, theological, and political roots and traditions. Such an exploration suggests that the central issue for Islam is its universalization. One may identify six partially overlapping positions, or schools of thought, within Islam today, each of which attempts to address the problem of Islamic unity. These positions are found among both U.S. adversaries and partners in current overseas contingency operations.

Islam today is far from monolithic. It is manifested in many forms, reflecting multiple perspectives on how the faith is to achieve its universalization, on what *jihad* means, and on when, if ever, terrorist tactics are justifiable in defense of Islam. Traditionalist conceptions of Islam maintain the continuing applicability of *Shari'ah* as state law, and the potentiality for *jihad* as warfare, with an average of over 20 percent of Muslims in Muslim-majority nations finding terrorist acts at times justifiable in defense of Islam. Liberal and post-modern reformists, on the other hand, generally condemn violent *jihad* and seek peaceful relations with the West. An accurate assessment of Islam as power will inform that grand strategy and strategic vision on which effective national security policy rests.

A review of the national security policies of Presidents Bush and Obama demonstrates the incredible difficulty of bringing religion to bear within national security policy. To the alternative paradigms of Religion as Freedom and Religion as Unity, the author suggests a third, Religion as Ideology, arguing that it appears to offer the greatest utility. It calls for a strategic vision that comprehends the power of Islam, it enables a nuanced understanding of Islamic groups based on their behavior, it facilitates a diversified continuum of policy rewards and consequences based on that behavior, and it refrains from violating the American tradition of the Federal Government neither advocating for nor judging a religion.

If religion is to gain currency within national security policy, many practical matters will need to be addressed. For example, how should religion impact campaign design, campaign planning, and strategic communications with internal and external audiences? Relative to various positions within Islam, U.S. policymakers will need to understand the conceptions of universalization to which various Islamic positions aspire. Even more, policymakers will need to determine how much active support or passive space U.S. national interests can afford or allow toward the fulfillment of those aspirations. Knowing the parameters could amount to a national security imperative.

Finally, that religion will continue to matter, and matter a lot, in U.S. national security challenges may be a bitter pill for secularist western liberals to swallow. Certain political advisers, academics, and senior leaders of the professions of arms may find it difficult to believe that many 21st-century people are still motivated by religion, and that some are even willing to fight and die for their beliefs. Their incredulity is easy to document. National security policy statements, academic texts on cultural frameworks, and even military manuals on counterinsurgency doctrine can discuss their subject matter without examining religion as a power which motivates human behavior. The day has come to rethink assumptions and reengage in these critical arenas.

THE ROLE OF RELIGION
IN NATIONAL SECURITY POLICY
SINCE SEPTEMBER 11, 2001

INTRODUCTION

When it comes to formulating national security policy today, religion may be regarded as the elephant in the room—we all know it is there, but nobody really wants to talk about it.[1] On one hand, some U.S. policymakers and advisers have had concerns about granting religion a place at the table because its subject matter might not be appropriate. On the other hand, those who have been struggling to find a way to integrate religion into the post-September 11, 2001 (9/11) discussion of national security have not yet found a fully satisfactory framework.

For some people, the perceived subjectivity of religion makes it an inappropriate element for national security policy. Some view religion as mere subjective preference, shaping personal choices about God and right and wrong. By contrast, they view national security policy as objective decision making, employing elements of national power against a real adversary. Consider, however, Sun Tzu's strategic dictum: "Know the enemy and know yourself; in a hundred battles you will never be in danger."[2] Here the so-called subjectivity-objectivity polarity collapses in favor of a subject-object distinction: know your enemy and know yourself. What is such knowledge other than the perception of deeply rooted identity, values, interests, and sources of power which, more often than not, touch on, or even flow from, religious traditions?

Others dissent from including religion within national security policy out of concern for compromising what many call the American separation of Church and State. Because religion is spiritual, promoting an inner life springing from God they argue, would it not be improper for the United States to speak to religion within its national security policy? Carl von Clausewitz's anthropological framework for war suggests otherwise. In his paradoxical trinity, people supply the emotions and passions of war.[3] Because human emotions and passions are frequently founded on religion, why wouldn't national security policy discuss the motivational power and effects of religion?

Still others judge religion to be too privatistic and idealistic to contribute anything meaningful in the national security world of deadly force and cut-and-thrust maneuvering. We must remember, however, that this is a distinctively liberal, western view that conceives of religion as a private affair divorced from daily life. Most societies see religion as related to individual identity, societal formation, and national values. Religion provides humanity with a framework for understanding the world, human meaning, and human conflict. Religion, of necessity, speaks to war and its conduct.[4]

In his masterpiece, *The Quest for Holiness*, Adolf Köberle sets forth the trajectories of the various world religions in their attempts to fulfill the human aspiration to overcome the pathos of this world. Köberle identifies this aspiration as humanity's desire for sanctification—for acceptance and holiness before God.[5] His introduction reads like a primer on human need, which can drive to violence and perpetuate human conflict, and, in that sense, like an introduction to the problem of national security.

1

> The desire for sanctification is always first aroused in man when he has become conscious, in some painful way, of his lack of peace and the erring restlessness of his life. So the experiences of age and suffering, of sickness and death that surround us. . . . the realization of our moral weakness and uncleanliness, the continually repeated neglect of our duties toward our neighbor awakens a desire for supernatural strength and purity. . . . These are the momentous hours when we have come to the point that secular values can no longer satisfy us; when the need of aspiring to God is recognized and we unite in the longing cry that is the hidden theme of all human history: "Dona nobis pacem."[6]

That religion and national security policy largely share a common base—the experience of human suffering, failed duties toward one's neighbor, the hunger for enduring values, and the desire for peace—suggests an integrative approach for religion within national security policy. How though, should religion and national security policy be integrated? If there is a place at the table for religion, where should it sit?

If religion is to enter the discussion, it must not do so in the form of advocacy, promoting one religion over another.[7] Nor may it do so in the form of judgment, ruling on the orthodoxy or heterodoxy of a religion. Rather, religion must enter the discussion in the form of behavior.

Behavior matters—whether it is motivated by religious faith, nationalist commitment, or an empty stomach. Because behavior can support U.S. interests or attack them, protect innocents or take their lives, our security requires that we understand behavior. Religion is critically needed now in our national security discussions. We need to understand more clearly the way that religion can shape and motivate behavior. When it comes to our security, the behavior of our friends and our adversaries matters terribly.

Religion—not as a standard of belief, but as a power which drives human behavior—must be at the table if national security policy is to embrace the fullness of the human situation, formulate effective concepts, and yield enduring results. There is room for both a more nuanced consideration and a more comprehensive treatment of religion in U.S. national security policy. We need a workable framework that will provide such nuance and integration.

The struggle to locate this framework has taken the United States down a number of roads since the turn of the millennium, none of which has been totally satisfactory. President George W. Bush viewed freedom as a universal value, with religion as the preeminent freedom characterizing free, robust societies. With these assumptions, he viewed the post-9/11 conflict with the Taliban and al-Qaeda as a battle over freedom. He believed that repressed Iraqis and Afghans would welcome the U.S. military as liberators bringing greater freedom, to include freedom of religion. His assumptions were only partially validated. Part of the problem was the dissonance between a western concept of freedom to choose and worship God, over against an Islamic concept to submit to God. Religion as Freedom did not offer the optimal framework.

Neither has President Barack Obama's Religion as Unity framework solved the problem. Obama has asserted a universal value regarding religion—that all religions are united by a moral law to care for one's fellowman. Based on this assumption, Obama has labeled terrorists as false Muslims, and has launched initiatives to honor Islam and resolve mutual misunderstandings through dialog with Muslim states. His efforts have succeeded partially, but radical traditionalist Muslims continue to fight, believing they are the pure practitioners of the faith. Also, Obama's framework has not accounted for the large numbers of Muslims in Muslim-majority countries who at times find terrorism to be justifiable.

An additional framework is needed, one that understands religion as power which is comprehended in grand strategy, and religion as behavior which is addressed in policy. This manuscript proposes to locate that framework by examining the role of religion in national security policy since 9/11, dividing the topic into four sections.[8] The first section helps define the potential scope of the interplay of religion and national security by projecting the question into the future. The works of four recent historiographers are examined, with special attention to their visions of the current and future world, and the role of religion with regards to human conflict.[9]

Because the United States is currently engaged in conflicts in Iraq and Afghanistan—both Islamic countries—the second section provides an excursus on the power of Islam. As the religion of the Taliban and al Qaeda, but also of Egypt, Jordan, Saudi Arabia, and many other U.S. allies, Islam is *the* religion under discussion today in matters of national security. The power of Islam is explored by examining its history, different forms of *jihad*, various approaches to achieving Islamic unity, alignments within radical Islam and terrorist operations, and demographics that bear on Islamic identity and the extent of support for terrorism.

The role of religion within the national security policies of Presidents Bush and Obama are discussed in the third section. Based on their approaches, two paradigms for integrating religion within national security policy, Religion as Freedom and Religion as Unity, are evaluated. A third paradigm, Religion as Ideology, is offered in an attempt to relate a strategic vision which comprehends the power of Islam to be capable of translating policy into religious behavior.

The fourth section provides a summary and addresses certain practical questions that would need to be answered if the United States moves toward a comprehensive framework for religion using the paradigm of Religion as Ideology. What changes might occur at the strategic and operational levels of war? What might be the way ahead?

I. HISTORIOGRAPHICAL PROJECTIONS ON HUMAN CONFLICT AND RELIGION

To understand the interplay between religion and national security, one may either look backwards across history to assess past connections, or forward from today to project future connections.[10] I have chosen the latter, as this allows an anchor point in the current, but evolving, geopolitical world, with its well-known national security challenges.

The four authors surveyed—Alvin Toffler, Francis Fukuyama, Samuel Huntington, and Robert Kaplan—have proposed perhaps the most compelling alternative visions of the future world written in the past 30 years. Each advances his own paradigm, through which he offers a distinctive view of history and projects a future world.[11] To a greater or lesser extent, each author discusses his understanding of the causes and projected occurrences of violent conflict, and the attendant role of religion. This survey is included, not to critique their works nor to claim that their works were written to prove a connection between religion and national security interests. Rather, this overview is included to explore the relationship between religion and human conflict, within a set of possible futures, in order to project back a present-day azimuth for national security policy alternatives that consider the role of religion.

Alvin Toffler.[12]

In his 1980 book, *The Third Wave*, Alvin Toffler pictures humanity's struggle as the quest to absorb change and to craft a related ideology that offers meaning for the new reality. For Toffler, humanity has experienced three "waves" of change—first agriculture; second, industry; and third, super technology—each of which has radically altered civilizational self-understanding, societal practices, and personal meaning. The rise of agriculture 10,000 years ago brought the First Wave.[13] The industrial revolution signaled the Second Wave.[14] Now, a Third Wave has arisen, marked by technological innovation, data systems, decentralized media, renewable energy, invisible economies, chaos theory, fragmented values, and accelerated change.[15]

Toffler locates the seeds of human conflict within his concept of wave confluence. Confluence occurs when a new wave crashes into the previous wave, producing a new situation, a new synthesis, a new civilization. Such new civilizations reflect more than paradigm shifts for ordinary societal labor—from agriculture to industry to technological science. More critically, every new civilization "develops its own 'super-ideology' to explain reality and justify its own experience."[16]

According to Toffler, struggle is the inevitable result of two waves crashing together, each with its own super-ideology. For him, this explains the violent conflict, within states and between states, that occurred at the confluence of the First and Second Waves.[17] Similarly, as the Second and Third Waves collide:

> The decisive struggle today is between those who try to prop up and preserve industrial society [Second Wave] and those who are ready to advance beyond it [Third Wave]. This is the super-struggle for tomorrow.
>
> Other, more traditional conflicts between classes, races, and ideologies will not vanish. They may even—as suggested earlier—grow more violent, especially if we undergo large-scale economic turbulence. But all these conflicts will be absorbed into, and play themselves out within, the super-struggle as it rages through every human activity.[18]

This decisive struggle is intensified because the Third Wave has brought tremendous ideological challenges, including religious challenges. In the Second Wave, the typical citizen retained long-term commitments aligned with the majority.[19] In the Third Wave, civilization "makes allowances for individual difference, and embraces (rather than suppresses) racial, regional, religious, and subcultural variety."[20] The resultant stress is "tearing our families apart . . . shattering our values."[21] Toffler notes that this shift in ground rules has led many to pursue fundamentalist religion to find, "something—almost anything—to believe in,"[22] and to join religious cults in order to locate, "community, structure, and meaning."[23]

In short, Toffler treats the subject of religion not as a body of beliefs, but as a manifestation of the confluence of Second and Third Wave ideologies; not as a source of absolute truth, but as a proof of the fragmented values of Third Wave civilization; not as a majority-based morality to guide society, but as a pattern of minority-based power within society.[24] This reading of Toffler suggests that religion—especially as fleshed out in fragmented, smaller faith communities—will become increasingly vocal and powerful. Effective Third Wave governments will include religious groups as stakeholders, much as they would any minority power base within their ruling coalition.

The policy implication for Toffler seems to be that it is wiser to include religion as a dynamic, societal force, than to omit it and risk irrelevancy or failure. Indeed, his interpretation of the 1979 Iranian Revolution offers a good illustration of how Third Wave national security policy may ignore religion only to its great peril:

> Nurtured by the West, attempting to apply the Second Wave strategy . . . [the pre-revolution] Teheran government conceived of development as a basically economic process. Religion, culture, family life, sexual roles—all these would take care of themselves if only the dollar signs were got right. . . . Despite certain unique circumstances—like the combustive mixture of oil and Islam—much of what happened in Iran was common to other countries pursuing the Second Wave strategy.[25]

Francis Fukuyama.[26]

In his 1992 book, *The End of History and the Last Man*, Francis Fukuyama embarks on a brave journey to locate a universal history of mankind. Toward this end, he seeks to determine the evoutionary engines of human history, identify tensions within the unfolding of the historical process, consider implications for his philosophical construal of anthropology and community, and project a provisional end state for humanity.[27] Based on an optimistic philosophy of history and borrowing heavily from Georg Wilhelm Friedrich Hegel,[28] Fukuyama traces the evolution of systems of human governance, in the light of the human condition, and tracks a path leading to universal liberal democracy.[29] This would represent the end of history, i.e., its final, rational goal and manifestation.[30]

The historical process that would lead to universal liberal democracy, Fukuyama maintains, runs on the twin engines of economics and the human struggle for recognition. The former represents the simpler case for Fukuyama, given the power of technology and the "universal horizon of economic production possibilities."[31] The latter is more complex. Man's desire to be recognized as possessing dignity and worth—in particular, his desire to be recognized as *desirable*, i.e., recognized as greater than his fellow man—has led to an historical chain of slave and master identities, and to war itself.[32] Within this construct, Fukuyama finds religion, and also nationalism and other forms of ideology, to be penultimate fulfillments of the human struggle for recognition.[33] Because religion can end up perpetuating slave and master identities,[34] it presents an obstacle to forming liberal democracies, which alone give full expression to the non-negotiable principles of "liberty and equality."[35]

Fukuyama admits his historical method and anthropological assumptions generate analytical problems as humanity nears the final destination of history. If humanity and society separate themselves from their ideological foundations and commitments, how will this affect their ability to sustain themselves internally and engage the world externally? It is to this question we now turn, briefly considering difficulties in the areas of anthropology, sociology, and international relations. This line of inquiry will help sketch a preliminary picture of the role of religion and national security implications in Fukuyama's projected future.

On the anthropological side, Fukuyama believes that the most probable danger is that "the creature who reportedly emerges at the end of history, the *last man*,"[36] will lose his passions, his ability to strive, and cease to be a true man. Having been indoctrinated that the birthright of every human is absolute freedom and absolute equality at absolutely no personal cost, the last man will have lost the capacity to make ultimate commitments and, therein, his capacity to be human.[37] Fukuyama also warns of the opposite, less likely, danger: humanity jettisoning the entire project of liberal democracy due to its loss of absolutes. Religion, nationalism, and ideologies would then drive a history which had not ended, and whose demise had been prematurely projected.[38]

On the sociological side, within the United States those private associations which previously enabled debate and built strength within liberal democracies would be so emptied of religion and other ideological causes that the public good, as the politically-negotiated coherence of privately-held rights, might well collapse.[39] Where tolerance requires being open to all belief systems, it unavoidably attacks the normative character of any one system. Fukuyama's surprising solution is to re-empower personal ideology, to include religion, to make liberalism sustainable. He argues:

> No fundamental strengthening of community life will be possible unless individuals give back certain of their rights to communities, and accept the return of certain historical forms of intolerance. . . . Men and women who made up American society . . . were for the most part members of religious communities held together by a common moral code and belief in God. . . . Liberal principles had a corrosive effect on the values predating liberalism necessary to sustain strong communities, and thereby on a liberal society's ability to be self-sustaining.[40]

Regarding international relations, because societies and states are located at different distances from the end of history[41] — with some still retaining robust religious, nationalist, and cultural ideologies — the United States would still need to practice foreign relations, so as to engage the power of religion in those lesser developed societies where it remains the decisive, or at least a not-yet-marginalized, power.[42] Here Fukuyama singles out the Islamic world.

> At the end of history, there are no serious ideological competitors left to liberal democracy. . . . Outside the Islamic world, there appears to be a general consensus that accepts liberal democracy's claims to be the most rational form of government.[43]

For Fukuyama, Islam would seem to merit special attention in national security policy. He represents Islam as an ideology that attracts those who are already "culturally Islamic,"[44] that possesses "its own code of morality and doctrine of political and social justice,"[45] and that has "defeated liberal democracy in many parts of the Islamic world, posing a grave threat to liberal practices even in countries where it has not achieved political power directly."[46]

To sum up, these difficulties seem to suggest a conclusion that runs counter to the overall direction of Fukuyama's thesis. My reading of Fukuyama is that his projected post-historical United States would, of necessity, retain religion as a power within society and as a lens for addressing national security issues for that society. Religion would thus remain a critical component of effective foreign policy in Fukuyama's future world to meet the challenges of external threats, internal associations, and enduring anthropological distinctions.

Samuel P. Huntington.[47]

In his 1996 book, *The Clash of Civilizations and the Remaking of World Order*, Samuel Huntington presents the case that the best paradigm for understanding and addressing current international conflict is the clash of civilizations. Prior to the fall of the Soviet Union, the alignment of world states was based chiefly on ideology, with states falling into "three blocs."[48] With the collapse of communism, however, Huntington finds that "culture and cultural identities, which at the broadest level are *civilization identities*, are shaping the patterns of cohesion, disintegration, and conflict."[49] Today,

> . . . [T]he most important distinctions among people are not ideological, political, or economic. They are cultural. . . . People define themselves in terms of ancestry, religion, language, history, values, customs, and institutions. They identify with cultural groups: tribes, ethnic groups, religious communities, nations, and, at the broadest level, civilizations.[50]

Identifying seven or eight such civilizations,[51] Huntington concludes that "in the emerging era, clashes of civilizations are the greatest threat to world peace, and an international order based on civilizations is the surest safeguard against world war."[52] Huntington calls such clashes "fault line wars."[53]

Religion plays two key roles within Huntington's paradigm. First, religion largely defines a civilization, and is usually its most important objective element.[54] Huntington quotes English historian Christopher Dawson: "The great religions are the foundations on which the great civilizations rest."[55] Second, because religion is so significant for defining civilizations, religion frequently serves as a critical driver in fault line wars.

Consider the religious components in Huntington's most likely and most dangerous fault line wars. At the micro level (localized wars), Huntington sees violent fault lines "between Islam and its Orthodox, Hindu, African, and Western Christian neighbors."[56] At the macro level (global wars), Huntington assesses the worst conflicts as occurring between Muslim and Asian societies on the one hand, and the West on the other. Overall, he projects that dangerous clashes (wars of greatest violence between states or entities from different civilizations) will result from the clash of "Western arrogance, Islamic intolerance, and Sinic [Chinese] assertiveness." Religion provides fuel for Huntington's future wars.[57]

Because Huntington explicitly names Islam as a civilization likely to clash in micro, macro, and dangerous wars, a further word is in order. Huntington reviews significant historical, political, cultural, and religious data as he makes his case for the likelihood of continued Islamic civilizational violence. His evidence may be grouped in three overlap-

7

ping areas: the Islamic Resurgence,[58] Islamic consciousness without cohesion, and the intercivilizational Islamic-western clash.

First, Huntington documents an Islamic Resurgence[59] wherein multitudes of Muslims have turned to Islam for:

> a source of identity, meaning, stability, legitimacy, development, power, and . . . hope epitomized in the slogan "Islam is the solution." . . . It embodies acceptance of modernity, rejection of Western culture, and recommitment to Islam as the guide to life in the modern world.[60]

He characterizes this Islamic resurgence as a mainstream and pervasive civilizational adjustment vis-à-vis the West, aimed at returning Muslims to "a purer and more demanding form of their religion."[61] Powerful demographic trends, such as large Islamic migrations to cities, exploding youth populations, and economic problems, have played no small part in this resurgence. Huntington believes that, although this resurgence will produce many social gains, it will leave unresolved "problems of social injustice, political repression, economic backwardness, and military weakness," thus fueling future conflict.[62]

Second, Huntington considers the implications of a strong, transnational Islamic consciousness that exists without cohesive power.[63] Huntington finds that traditional Islamic commitments to the family, the clan, and the tribe, as well as to unities of culture, religion, and empire, are producing a strong and widespread Islamic consciousness.[64] What is lacking today, however, is a core or lead state, or transnational power structure, to affect Islamic cohesion. The result has been instability through competition among aspiring Islamic states, sects, and transnational actors, each seeking to gain popular Muslim support to expand its own base and reach of power. For Huntington, this instability and competition increases the potential for conflict within Islamic civilization and between Islam and other civilizations.

Finally, Huntington addresses what he views as the basic clash of Islamic and Western civilizations.[65] Huntington tracks a stormy relationship between these civilizations across 1,400 years of history, with conflict flowing from, "the nature of the two religions and the civilizations based on them."[66] He documents that "the argument is made that Islam has from the start been a religion of the sword," that it has expanded by use of force when strong enough to do so, and that it has refused to grant equal protection under the law to adherents of other religions.[67] Beyond such historical and theological concerns, Huntington lists current trends which have contributed to the clash: increases in Islamic population, unemployment, and the number of disaffected youths; greater Islamic confidence over against the West through the Islamic Resurgence; the West's abrasive policies of universalizing its culture and meddling in conflicts in Islamic lands; the fall of communism, against which the West and Islam had made common cause; and increased intercivilizational contacts between Islam and the West, which have magnified intolerances between the two.[68] Huntington's view of the future is clear: religion as the preeminent cultural factor defining civilization will play a central role in any effective national security policy.[69]

Whatever the normative prejudices of the reader, whether one admits to the possibility of meaningful differences between religions and moral frameworks or not, the data

Huntington cites demonstrates points of friction between civilizations based on religion. It must be taken at a minimum as points of data regarding differences in human behavior, flowing from cultural differences between certain state, substate, and transnational identities. That such differences in behavior, irrespective of differences in belief, may lead to violence and war implies the criticality of addressing religion as behavior within national security policy.[70]

Robert Kaplan.[71]

In his 2000 book, *The Coming Anarchy: Shattering the Dreams of the Post Cold War*, Robert Kaplan advances his vision of the post-Cold War world, with special attention to U.S. national security implications. According to Kaplan, the Cold War brought significant order and stability to a world that was suspended between the polarities of U.S. and Soviet powers, tamping down fractious cultural, societal, and religious forces. Such forces, however, gained traction with the fall of the Soviet Union, destabilizing many countries and regions, and giving rise to "the coming anarchy." Within this context, Kaplan sees "the environment," as, "*the* national-security issue of the early twenty-first century."[72]

In Kaplan's coming anarchy, the population will largely be divided into the haves and the have nots based on the nature of the devolving world. Kaplan writes that "we are entering a bifurcated world," populated by Fukuyama's Last Man and Hobbes's First Man.[73] The former presents the few—post-modern humanity, which is well-educated, well-fed, dominant in technology, and successfully separated from the brutish world. The latter presents the many—entrapped humanity, which is surrounded by anarchy, living in poverty, engulfed in cultural strife, and doomed to failure by environmental privation.[74]

The polarities of Kaplan's future world imply that religion relates to concepts of security and stability in two different ways. First, Hobbes's First Man lives his brutish life in the throes of contradictory cultures, extremist ideologies, and religious constructs. For such a First Man, Kaplan's view is that although religion can sometimes be a positive force—contributing to individual empowerment, cultural identity, and societal order—more often religion is a negative force undermining stability and fueling conflict.

It is in this context that Kaplan discusses Islamic violence.[75] Although Kaplan sometimes interprets violence between Islamic peoples as springing from religious grounds, more frequently he perceives such Islamic violence as rising out of a cultural clash, with religion being subordinated to a specific Muslim culture. So it is that Turks may distrust and clash with Iranians, for example. That said, the cultural differences between Islam and the West are yet greater than the cultural differences within the House of Islam, so that in clashes between Islam and the West, a broader Muslim identity takes precedence.

This is not to suggest that Kaplan agrees with Huntington's thesis of a monolithic Islam clashing with western civilization.[76] Rather, Kaplan's view is that Huntington has oversimplified the matter and misidentified the clash. The clash is not between Islam and the West, but properly within Islam, or, more precisely, *within* the patchwork of competing *ethnic groups and cultures* which self-identify as Islamic; and then, only in a derived sense, between Islamic groups and cultures and the West.

But the role of religion in the life of the First Man is yet more complex. This is because Kaplan subordinates all such ethnic and cultural Islamic violence to his thesis of the coming anarchy. Kaplan describes "Islamic extremism [as] a psychological mechanism of many urbanized peasants threatened with the loss of traditions in pseudomodern cities where their values are under attack."[77] He sketches Islam as a religion bringing happiness to "millions of human beings in an increasingly impoverished environment,"[78] but whose "very militancy makes it attractive to the downtrodden. It is the one religion that is prepared to *fight*."[79] Thus, for Kaplan, foundational militancy within Islam is subordinated to the broader cultural identity, which, in turn, is subordinated to the environmental struggle of the First Man. From his perspective, the secular government of modern Turkey presents an outstanding success story of an Islamic culture driving toward moderation and modernity, effecting vital order and infrastructure within an Islamic society and "making it much harder for religious extremists to gain a foothold."[80]

Thus, in Kaplan's world of the First Man, religion will play a pivotal role in personal identity, cultural clashes, and the broader environmental struggle. Religion, especially as an enabler of culture, will empower the broader struggle seeking to gain control of critical resources, in hopes of securing a modicum of security and stability.

Second, consider Kaplan's appropriation of Fukuyama's Last Man. Although this suburbanized, well-fed, and self-satisfied man may have no *personal* need of religion, he will still have a *policy* need of religion; he will still need to influence the other strife-filled world where religion is valued, if only to achieve the ends of improved international stability and his own security. Kaplan makes the related policy point that the United States may have to learn to connect with cultures with which it holds little in common. It may sometimes be in the best interests of the United States to support authoritarian regimes in acute need of social stability and economic development, though not yet ready for democratic elections and still perpetuating systems of injustice.[81] Borrowing from James Madison in *The Federalist*, Kaplan suggests that American global engagement will likely best promote stability in fragile societies and governments by focusing on their regional, religious, and communal self-concern.[82] Thus, the Last Man's foreign policy will still need to address the priorities of the First Man, to include his religion.

Toffler, Fukuyama, Huntington, and Kaplan all articulate different visions of the current and future world, with varying views of national security challenges. Each author, however, includes religion as a critical component in policy that would address those challenges effectively, and highlights Islam within that process. Specifically how religion might be treated within national security policy—as a mark of freedom, a symbol of unity, or an expression of ideology—I address in section III.

II. THE POWER OF ISLAM

First, it is important to give some direct attention to the religion of Islam. This is necessary for at least three reasons: (1) Islamic terrorists attacked the United States on 9/11, (2) the Taliban and al Qaeda continue to use the religion of Islam as a rallying cry against the United States and the West, and (3) Pakistan, Egypt, Jordan, Saudi Arabia, and many other U.S. allies are Islamic countries.

These data points raise a particularly challenging question. How are Americans to comprehend the influence and the nature of a faith that is held by some of our most aggressive adversaries, but also by some of our most valued friends? This is the confusion that many Americans feel about Islam, and it is a confusion that cannot be clarified until we are willing to look more closely at the faith and its divisions.

That religions have divisions within them is not unusual. Judaism may be divided into Orthodox, Conservative, and Reformed. Christianity may be divided into Orthodox, Roman Catholic, Lutheran, Episcopal, Baptist, Methodist, Presbyterian, and many other denominations. What is unusual about Islam is that the divisions are extraordinarily complex and represent fundamentally different visions of how the faith is to achieve its universalization.

Yet we must understand Islam with its various divisions if we are to understand Islam as a power which motivates behavior. We must understand the faith dimension to derive the policy implication.[83]

Authoritative Documents.[84]

There are many approaches to studying Islam, but one helpful way is to begin with a review of its authoritative documents and then move to its history. Unlike Christianity, Islam emphasizes practice over belief, law over proclamation.[85] Accordingly, Islam considers its authoritative source documents as supremely important. The primary authority in Islam is the *Qur'an*, revealed from 610 to 632 of the Common Era (CE) and considered to be "the eternal, uncreated, literal word of God, revealed one final time to the Prophet Muhammad as a guide for humankind."[86] The *Qur'an* reveals information about Allah as the radically transcendent, divinely omnipotent and omniscient God, who alone is God, who in himself is Unity. However, the *Qur'an* does not reveal God, for God is beyond all grasp and comprehension. Rather, the *Qur'an* reveals God's universal will or law for all humanity.[87]

Stylistically, the *surahs*, or chapters, of the *Qur'an* are composed of dramatic and shifting forms, and not chronological narrative.[88] *Surahs* may be divided based on where the revelation was received—in Mecca or in Medina.[89]

The secondary authority in Islam is the *Sunnah*, composed of the words, deeds, and judgments of Mohammad, to include community practice flowing from the Prophet's example.[90] This form of customary law was written down by Muhammad's Companions, with the written documents themselves called *hadith*.[91] The *sirah*, or biographical accounts of Muhammad's life, also lie within the category of *Sunnah*.[92]

Together the *Qur'an* and *Sunnah* form the basis of divine law, called *Shari'ah*.[93] Meaning "straight path," *Shari'ah* is that law in Islam that effects the rule of God and governs life—individual, community, and state. *Shari'ah* fuses the religious and civil worlds into one. *Shari'ah* is particularly instructive for the *ummah*, the one community of Islamic believers worldwide. *Shari'ah* tells the *ummah* what it means to be a Muslim.

A document of lesser, but still significant, authority in Islam is the *fatwa*, a formal restatement, or new application, of Islamic law. *Fatwas* are the result of difficulties both in understanding certain texts of the *Qur'an* and the *Sunnah*, and in applying those texts to new situations. Islamic legal scholars issue *fatwas* to address aspects of life ranging from prayer and discipline, to marriage and family, to war and politics. The perceived authority of a *fatwa* can depend on the faith community's respect for the scholar and his reasoning in matters of casuistry.

To enable resolution of interpretive difficulties, the Islamic legal tradition mushroomed. Principles of Islamic jurisprudence, or *usul al-fiqh*, established rules of interpretation, reasoning, precedence, and custom, in order to guide legal decisions.[94] *Siyar*, the Islamic law of nations, also developed, detailing the Islamic law of war. Five legal traditions crystallized. Based on texts from the *Qur'an* and *Sunnah* and the extensive legal system, *fatwas* became a standardized way for leading legal scholars to shape and apply Islamic law.[95]

Brief Overview of Islam.

The *Qur'an* documents a series of revelations to the Prophet Muhammad beginning in 610 CE.[96] After remaining silent for about 3 years, Muhammad went public and declared his revelations to the residents of Mecca. Decrying their polytheism and vices, he called for them to repent and submit fully to Allah, the one supreme Being. Following years of difficult preaching and persecution, Muhammad and a small band of followers migrated to Medina in 622. There Muhammad consolidated his religious and political power into one office, which he occupied as the singular spokesman and Prophet of God.

At Medina, Muhammad showed himself to be a wise and talented leader of the Medina community and his nascent *ummah*. The continuing revelations he received in Medina proved especially important for his religious and military future. Certain Medinan revelations to Muhammad established Islamic rites and practices as part of a universal religion. Other revelations authorized offensive military operations to achieve that vision. From Medina, Muhammad undertook a number of raids and battles against neighboring tribes, caravans, Jews, and a force of thousands from Mecca. The trend line multiplied Muhammad's power and wealth, and increased the number of those who submitted to Allah. The peaceful surrender of Mecca in 630 CE gave Muhammad undisputed control of the Arabian peninsula and religious hegemony based on his earlier order to expel all Christians and Jews. Before enacting a more expansive campaign to spread Islam through conquest, Muhammad fell ill and died in 632.

Following the death of Muhammad, the faithful demonstrated their resolve to realize their Prophet's universal vision of Islam. Islam experienced extensive growth by military conquest in the 7th and 8th centuries. Even through the 12th century, Islam continued to expand its rule, but it achieved this growth in an ebb-and-flow manner as European Christian powers began to achieve dominance. Still, at the height of its power Islam could claim Spain, parts of France and Italy, all of northern Africa, and large portions of Eurasia. That said, internal Islamic struggles for leadership, an ethos constrained by regimented commitment to the past, and the external European dynamism of the Renaissance, projected a final wall which Islam could not breech. Islam's defeat at the gates of Vienna on September 11-12, 1683, marked the end of Islam's linear, contiguous warfare to achieve universality. The vestiges of the great Ottoman Empire, launched in 1291, finally faded away through defeat in World War I. A new era for Islam had begun.

Before more thoroughly examining the claim that Islam initially expanded by military conquest in order to achieve its vision of universality, we must first note alternative views. Liberal scholarship and postmodern perspectives in the last century have articulated a transhistorical understanding of Islam's universality in exclusively internal, spiritual terms.[97] Other commentators have suggested that prudence precludes discussing a possible historical occurrence of Islamic militancy, to avoid aiding adversary recruitment or undercutting coalition building. Ibn Warraq sounds a cautionary note on bypassing history to satisfy ideology, especially one's own. Warraq quotes Isaiah Berlin, arguing that from the latent desire to, "suppress what [one] suspects to be true . . . has flowed much of the evil of this and other centuries."[98] From this perspective, the hard investigation of history provides the surest way to the flourishing of humanity.

Jihad.

The multiple interpretations of *jihad* that exist within Islam today contend both for legitimacy and adherents. The struggle over the definition of *jihad* is nothing less than the struggle over the defining character of Islam. Is the peace which Islam represents realized through external struggle, internal struggle, or a combination of the two? The original concept of *jihad* prioritized the meaning of *jihad* as external struggle or warfare, but included shadings of an internal or spiritual struggle. Changes in Islam's external operational environment led to an evolving concept of *jihad*.

This section documents the initial concept of *jihad* in Islam, its interpretation through the authoritative principles of Islamic jurisprudence, and its application within the Islamic war of nations. The following section traces modern interpretations of *jihad* that have arisen from reformed Islamic positions.

My reading of Islam's history, *usul al-fiqh* (principles of Islamic jurisprudence), *siyar* (the Islamic law of nations), and teaching on *jihad* (struggle or war) suggests that classical Islamic jurisprudence clearly accepted the proposition that Islam expanded by military conquest to achieve its goal of universality as envisioned by the Prophet.[99] To this, one may add that the early emphasis on militaristic or external *jihad* was joined by a rising accent on spiritual or internal *jihad*, as the initial and stunning military advances of Islam slowed.

Shaybani, born 750 CE, wrote Islam's most famous *siyar* detailing the authoritative understanding of the Islamic law of nations and classical Muslim notions of *jus ad bellum* and *jus in bello*. Shaybani's *siyar* demonstrates the historical and theological connection of *jihad* to the goal of achieving a universal Islamic state. Majid Khadduri, arguably the foremost authority on Shaybani, comments:

> The Islamic faith, born among a single people and spreading to others, used the state as an instrument for achieving a doctrinal or an ultimate religious objective, the proselytization of mankind. The Islamic state became necessarily an imperial and an expansionist state striving to win other peoples by conversion.[100]

13

Because the vision of a worldwide Islamic empire could not be achieved immediately, Islam needed to generate new law to govern the continued prosecution of war, the distribution of the spoils of war, and the relations of Islam with those states which had not yet been conquered. These necessities gave birth to *siyar* and defined its scope.

Based on this scope, *siyar* assumed a state of hostility between the Islamic and non-Islamic world. The world was divided into two parts: *dar al-Islam* (the territory of Islam) and *dar al-harb* (the territory of war).[101] *Dar al-Islam* was that part of the world ruled by *Shari'ah*, and *dar al-harb* was the military objective.

> The territory of war was the object, not the subject, of the Islamic legal system, and it was the duty of Muslim rulers to bring it under Islamic sovereignty whenever the strength was theirs to do so.[102]

This does not mean that *siyar* required continuous warfare against the *dar al-harb*. Although "the ultimate objective of Islam was the whole world," expediency or temporary Islamic weakness might justify the halting of hostilities and a temporary peace.[103] When opportunity arose, however, the Muslim ruler was expected to return to offensive operations and, by conquest, to achieve a universalization of Islam.

These offensive operations were, by definition, *jihad*. Khadurri notes:

> The instrument which would transform the *dar al-harb* into the *dar al-Islam* was the *jihad*. The *jihad* was not merely a duty to be fulfilled by each individual; it was also above all a political obligation imposed collectively upon the subjects of the state so as to achieve Islam's ultimate aim—the universalization of the faith and establishment of God's sovereignty over the world.[104]

Hamidullah clarifies an important point. *Jihad* was not to be considered an individual duty in an absolute sense, but only in a derived sense, for *jihad* belonged to the state:

> *Jihad* is not considered as a personal duty to be observed by each and every individual, but only a general duty which, if accomplished by a sufficient number, the rest will no more be condemned for the neglect of that duty—this fact renders the administration of *jihad* entirely in the hands of the government. The practice of the Prophet also shows the same thing.[105]

Such an understanding of *jihad* as state-sponsored, chiefly offensive military operations raises eyebrows today. Liberal and postmodern reformed accounts of Islam largely bypass documentary and historical evidence from the initial centuries of Islam in favor of emphasizing Islam as a religion that has expanded through the attraction of its inherently peaceful, spiritual discipline.

There is some evidence for each side, but most *Qur'anic* verses on *jihad* refer to actual fighting. Consider the following:

> Indeed, Allah has purchased from the believers their lives and their properties [in exchange] for that they will have Paradise. They fight in the cause of Allah, so they kill and are killed. [It is] a true promise [binding] upon Him. . . . Rejoice in your transaction.[106]

When the sacred months have passed, then kill the polytheists wherever you find them and capture them and besiege them and sit in wait for them at every place of ambush. But if they should repent, establish prayer, and give *zakah* [alms], let them [go] on their way. Indeed, Allah is Forgiving and Merciful.[107]

Fight those who do not believe in Allah or in the Last Day and who do not consider unlawful what Allah and His Messenger have made unlawful and who [Jews and Christians] do not adopt the religion of truth. . . . [Fight] until they give the *jizyah* [annual tax] willingly while they are humbled.[108]

Not equal are those believers remaining [at home] . . . [compared to] the *mujahideen*, [who strive and fight] in the cause of Allah with their wealth and their lives. Allah has preferred the *mujahideen* through their wealth and their lives over those who remain [behind] . . . Allah has preferred the *mujahideen* over those who remain [behind] with a great reward.[109]

And fight them until there is no *fitnah* [sedition or idolatry] and [until] the religion, all of it, is for Allah. And if they cease — then indeed, Allah is Seeing of what they do.[110]

To the above verses we must add the authoritative example of the Prophet, in support of understanding *jihad* as war. From the time he arrived at Medina until his death, Muhammad was a warrior. When words and other actions could not convince or coerce non-Muslims to submit to him as the Prophet of Allah, he regularly used warfare to advance Islam. Sometimes such warfare was brutal. Muhammad's role in ratifying the 627 CE beheading of between 600-800 captured Jewish men is well documented in the *hadith*.[111] His farewell address in March of 632 reflected a similar understanding of *jihad*: "I was ordered to fight all men until they say 'There is no god but Allah'."[112]

On the other side, there are *Qur'anic* verses, although significantly fewer, which emphasize *jihad* as a spiritual, inner struggle or striving. Examples include the following:

And strive for Allah with the striving due to Him. He has chosen you and has not placed upon you in the religion any difficulty. [It is] the religion of your father, Abraham. Allah named you "Muslims" before [in former scriptures] and in this [revelation] that the Messenger may be a witness over you and you may be witnesses over the people. So establish prayer and give *zakah* [alms] and hold fast to Allah. He is your protector; and excellent is the protector, and excellent is the helper.[113]

Those who remained behind rejoiced in their staying [at home] after [the departure of] the Messenger of Allah and disliked to strive with their wealth and their lives in the cause of Allah and said "Do not go forth in the heat." Say "The fire of Hell is more intensive in heat."[114]

There shall be no compulsion in [acceptance of] the religion. The right course has become clear from the wrong. So whoever disbelieves in *Taghut* and believes in Allah has grasped the most trustworthy handhold with no break in it. And Allah is Hearing and Knowing.[115]

To these verses we must also add the later distinction of the greater *jihad* and the lesser *jihad*. In the 9th century, ascetic impulses within Islam began to merge into a mystical interpretation — Sufism — generating some documentation of a new distinction between a greater and lesser *jihad*. Although such documentation is absent from the authoritative *hadith*, 9th century wisdom literature provides examples:

> A number of fighters came to the Messenger of Allah, and he said: "You have done well in coming from the 'lesser *jihad*' to the 'greater *jihad*'." They said: "What is the 'greater *jihad*'?" He said: "For the servant [of God] to fight his passions."[116]

We must note that there need not be a contradiction, strictly speaking, between the belligerent and irenic passages of the *Qur'an*; *jihad* may entail both.[117] That said, there is undeniable dissonance between the *Qur'anic* passages which portray *jihad* as state-sponsored, offensive warfare used to expand Islam and achieve universality on the one hand, and *jihad* as inner, spiritual striving used to build Islam through peaceful, spiritual discipline. The Islamic legal tradition of *usul al-fiqh* helps in part to resolve this dissonance.

Within *usul al-fiqh*, the principle of *naskh* (abrogation) allows certain later passages of the *Qur'an* and elements of *Shari'ah* to take precedence over earlier passages or elements.[118] This resolution rules out contradiction. Instead, based on the relative time of the revelations, the latter takes precedence over the former. In this way *naskh* has been used by some commentators to argue that the later, Medinan exhortations to wage war against infidels take precedence over and abrogate the earlier Meccan requirements to pursue only peaceful means.[119] Terrorist Muslims continue to use *naskh* in this way as the basis in *Shari'ah* for their terrorist *fatwas*.[120] Other modern commentators reject *naskh* to embrace earlier Islamic admonitions of peace.

The Central Question for Islam—How Islam Is to Achieve its Universalization.

This brief study of Islam, pivoting on historical periods of peace and war, and on alternative understandings of *jihad*, suggests that the problem of Islam is the problem of unity.[121] Islamic unity begins and ends within Allah, who is uniquely and radically one in himself, transcendent beyond humanity and the world. Through the *Qur'an* and the testimony of the Prophet, God has given his divine law—*Shari'ah*—as the means for establishing his rule among humanity. Only in full submission to Allah, through obedience to his *Shari'ah*, can there be peace.[122] Although the *ummah* and their *dar al-Islam* know this peace, *dar al-harb* does not. This presents a problem, for it is the will of the transcendent God, who himself is Unity, that all submit to him. Within the classical construction, only when *dar al-Islam* overcomes *dar al-harb* and places it under *Shari'ah*, will God's command be met and permanent peace realized.

In the initial stages of Islam, militant *jihad* was a critical component of life under *Shari'ah*. *Dar al-Islam* conquered large portions of *dar al-harb*, bringing *Shari'ah* to an ever-widening kingdom, but as the expansionist victories of Islam subsided, the realization of the Islamic vision of universality became problematic. A new approach to Islamic unity—other than military conquest to establish worldwide *Shari'ah*—seemed necessary. An evolving reality brought modifications to the previous *jihad* construct and to relations between Islamic and other states.

Below, I identify six partially overlapping positions, or schools of thought, within Islam today, each of which attempts to address the problem of Islamic unity. These positions are found among both U.S. adversaries and partners in current overseas contingency operations. Understanding these positions is a vital starting point for resolving related conflict and national security issues.

My study of Islam suggests that Islam's historic vision of its own universalization assumed that *Shari'ah* would one day rule all lands, that *usul al-fiqh* would remain authoritative for regulating the analysis of the legal sources and deducing the content of Islamic law, and that *jihad* as warfare would remain a legitimate mechanism to universalize Islam.[123] Relative to this historic three-fold vision, I identify six positions within Islam today.[124] Those groups which retain this vision, albeit with some conditions and concessions to reality, I call traditionalists. I find three categories of traditionalists: radical, conservative, and neotraditionalist Muslims. Those groups which have left the traditionalist understanding, yet articulate another principle of Islamic unity that they apply to public and political life, I label reformists. I denominate two categories of reformists: postmodern and liberal. Finally, those groups which have retained allegiance to Islam as authoritative for personal faith and practice, yet reject any role of Islam in the political sphere, I refer to as secular-state Muslims. See Table 1 for a summary of the related nomenclature.[125]

Full Name of Islamic Position	Shortened Name of Position	Name of Adherents
Radical Traditionalist Islam	Radical Islam	Radical Muslims
Conservative Traditionalist Islam	Conservative Islam	Conservative Muslims
Neotraditionalist Islam	N/A	Neotraditionalist Muslims
Postmodern Reformed Islam	Postmodern Islam	Postmodern Muslims
Liberal Reformed Islam	Liberal Islam	Liberal Muslims
Secular-State Islam	N/A	Secular-State Muslims

Table 1. Islamic Positions.

Radical traditionalist Islam generally sees no need to change from Islam's historic assumptions regarding the universalization of the faith. Radical Islamic groups desire a return to Islam as it was practiced in its first centuries, seeking the expansion of Islam through *Shari'ah*, applying *usul al-fiqh*, and leaving open the possibility of militant *jihad*.

The roots of radical Islam as a revivalist movement were sown by the 18th century work of Muhammad ibn abd al-Wahhab, the 1979 Islamic Revolution in Iran led by *Shi'i* Ayatollah Ruhollah Khomeni, and the 20th century evolution of Salafism as a movement containing increasing numbers of radical Muslims.[126] Today, radical Muslims are present around the world and affiliated with scores of Islamic groups and countries, to include *Shi'is* from Hezbbollah and Iran, and *Sunnis* from Hamas, Fatah al-Islam, the Taliban, al-Qaeda, and other Wahhabist derivatives, to name but a very few.[127] Radical Muslims frequently demonstrate hostility not only toward the West, but also toward those Muslims whom they judge to be apostate or corrupted.[128]

It is important to distinguish radical Islam from terrorism. As a defined group, radical Muslims are not all terrorists. That said, many within this group are terrorists.[129] By terrorists, I mean those who aim violence against innocents, in order to create fear and advance their political ends.

The use of terror as a tactic is highly problematic within the Islamic tradition. *Qur'an* 2:195 and 4:29 are often quoted as proof that terrorist suicide operations are forbidden in Islam.[130] Cook, however, cites a number of Islamic legal rulings and *Qur'anic* verses used by terrorists to argue just the opposite. Terrorist radical Muslims distinguish between suicide operations and martyrdom operations, and view martyrdom as a way to leverage minimal resources to achieve both maximum damage against the enemy, and eternal reward for the martyr.[131]

Conservative traditionalist Islam shares with radical Islam similar commitments to *Shari'ah*, *usul al-fiqh*, and *jihad*, but makes greater concessions to geopolitical realities. Here one finds a realist perspective on traditionalism. Khadduri is in many ways representative of such conservative Muslims. He seeks no reevaluation of the *Qur'an* and *Sunnah*, and no reformulation of *Shari'ah*, for he is content with the traditionally deduced law. He does, however, make concessions for Islamic nations vis-à-vis the international community and the power of the West. He argues that, just as *jihad* evolved from imperialist expansion to defensive war due to the growing strength of adversaries, even so the Islamic principle of unity has had to evolve.[132] Khadduri tracks an accompanying change from the goal of a universal Islamic state to a system of Islamic nations no longer at permanent war with the West to the goal of an Islamic bloc of nations in common cause cooperating within the community of nations.[133] Here, we find a conservative vision of unity founded not in Westphalian nationalism, but in the *ummah* living under *Shari'ah*, and united with fellow-Muslims of other Islamic nation states. Conservative Muslim approaches to unity may be found in Pakistan, Afghanistan, and many other Islamic nation states.

Neotraditionalist Islam also values *Shari'ah*, *usul al-fiqh*, and *jihad* within the historic Islamic tradition, but seeks to readjudicate the goals and objectives of *Shari'ah*, to better integrate Islam in the present. Like conservatives, neotraditionalists frequently envision the unity of Islam in terms of an Islamic bloc of nations together addressing the community of nations. But going beyond this, neotraditionalist Muslims seek an updated integration of Islamic tradition within their respective societies.

Mohammad Hashim Kamali well represents the neotraditionalist Muslim position. His assessment is that over time *usul al-fiqh* became "a retrospective construct," and "a theoretical, rather than empirical, discipline."[134] Over time, it fell short of "integrating the time-space factor into the fabric of its methodology."[135] As a result, *usul al-fiqh* became literalistic, wooden, and incapable of bringing the original dynamism of the *Qur'an* and the *Sunnah* forward into present Islamic culture and society. Kamali calls for a reevaluation of these sacred texts to capture anew:

18

> . . . their emphasis on justice, equality and truth, on commanding good and forbidding evil, on the promotion of benefit and prevention of harm, on charity and compassion, on fraternity and co-operation among the tribes and nations of the world, on consultation and government under the rule of law.[136]

Many Islamic movements may be described as neotraditionalist. These include the Muslim Brotherhood organizations found in many Islamic states, the Renaissance Party of Tunisia, the Islamic Salvation Front of Algeria, the Jamaat-i-Islami found in Pakistan and Bangladesh, and others.[137] It is significant that although such organizations may be designated as neotraditionalist, their "neo" status does not preclude their potential support for militant *jihad*.[138]

Reformed positions within Islam conceive of a different approach to the unity of the faith. While retaining a high view of the *Qur'an* and *Sunnah*, reformed Islam distinguishes between sacred traditions which may be anchored in historical conditions, and enduring principles and values which may be projected across time into the present. Therefore, reformed Islam accepts only nonviolent concepts of *jihad* and seeks fuller integration within a globalized western world.

Postmodern reformed Islam finds clear expression in the work of Tariq Ramadan.[139] Many proponents of postmodern Islam focus on the Muslim experience in the West, and Ramadan is a good example. Ramadan's goal is to articulate and apply universal principles for Islam which both respect pluralism, and enable Muslims to live out their faith in modern secular societies.[140] Based on his interpretation of Islamic sources and sciences, Ramadan identifies "three fundamentals of the universal at the heart of Islamic civilization," namely "the encounter with the Only One, the 'full and natural faith' of the created universe, [and] the 'need of Him' as the essence of being human."[141] These fundamentals bring changed conceptions of *Shari'ah* and *jihad*, and shift the concept of Islamic unity from the external to the internal.[142] This unity occurs first within the individual Muslim. First "to be with God . . . all of us are required to return to ourselves and to rediscover the original breath, to revive it and confirm it."[143] From here, this unity is projected into society, because "one's *duty* before God is to respond to the *right* of human beings."[144] This solidarity with society propels postmodern Muslims into a program of engagement for the right to life and the minimum necessary to sustain it, the right to family, the right to housing, the right to education, the right to work, the right to justice, and the right to solidarity itself.[145] From the postmodern Muslim perspective, this oneness, founded in the individual and projected into society, forms the basis of the universalized Islamic civilization.[146]

Liberal reformed Islam provides a vision similar to that of postmodern Islam, valuing the *Qur'an* and *Sunnah*, seeking enduring Islamic principles and values, and pursuing reform in the context of an increasingly modernized world. Beyond this, however, liberal Islam interprets the whole of the faith within the overarching categories of religious process and religious continuity. We will briefly examine both of these categories from the perspective of John L. Esposito, an ardent and articulate proponent of reformed Islam.[147]

Esposito locates Islam within the category of religious process in such a way that the historical underpinnings of the faith give way to deeper meanings which extend both backward and forward in time.[148] Islam at its emergence was "a return to a forgotten faith."[149] As such, Islam was "not a new faith but the restoration of the true faith (*iman*), a *process* that required the reformation of an ignorant, deviant society."[150] Part of this reformation entailed *jihad*, a "struggle against oppression and unbelief," which provides Muslims today "with a model and ideology for protest, resistance, and revolutionary change."[151] In short, Islam possesses a "transhistorical significance . . . rooted in the belief that the Book and the Prophet provide eternal principles and norms on which Muslim life, both individual and collective, is to be patterned."[152]

Esposito also portrays Islam as participating in a great phenomenological continuity of world religion. Esposito praises what he perceives Islam, Judaism, and Christianity to hold in common—a heritage of monotheism, spiritual values, and peaceful proclamation.[153]

One might ask: What kind of reform will liberal Islam bring, having been formed by religious process and continuity and normed by enduring Islamic principles and values? The answers will vary based on the realities of each Muslim society, but the process of contextualizing Islam within a globalized world will finally expand justice for Muslims across the domains of gender, economy, law, and politics, as Esposito sees it. As might be expected, western governments laud this vision and cheer the process.

Finally, secular-state Islam reflects that position which retains allegiance to Islam as authoritative for personal faith and practice, but rejects the role of religion in the political sphere. Egypt and Turkey are two such secular states and have attempted to travel the difficult road to modernity while honoring Islamic piety. Significant challenges continue today.[154] Their societies view *Shari'ah* as applicable for the private and community practice of Islam, and as decisive for the true unity of Islam across the *ummah*. That said, *Shari'ah* remains officially excluded from the power relationships of government. In other words, although Islamic principles may permeate law, *Shari'ah* itself is not state law, and is not determinative for state relations. Based on this understanding of private faith practice and secular political power, Egypt and Turkey have found common cause with the United States and other Western nations, and are vital partners within the community of nations.

To summarize, the above six schools of thought represent varying approaches to the practice of Islam today. Most significantly, each position holds its own view on how the Islamic faith is to achieve its universalization. Understanding these positions is a prerequisite for policymakers who would address national security issues in the Islamic world, but to this understanding we must also add an awareness of the changing nature of coalitions within traditionalist Islam.

Alignments within Traditionalist Islam.

Common wisdom in the West previously assumed that the chief divide within Islam was between *Sunnis* and *Shi'is*. Whereas this may well remain true theologically, this is not necessarily the case regarding national security. As we have seen, positions within traditionalist Islam—radical, conservative, and neotraditionalist—remain open to the potential legitimacy of *jihad* as warfare, whereas reformed Islam rejects violent *jihad*. This would suggest that the most significant divide within Islam is between the traditionalist and reformed positions, but the situation is yet more complex. Recent research shows that some traditionalist *Sunnis* and *Shi'is* align themselves together against the West, while other *Sunnis* and *Shi'is* find common cause against other *Sunnis*, notwithstanding the enduring differences in motivation and strategy which obtain between *Sunnis* and *Shi'is*.

Thomas F. Lynch III notes important differences in motivation and strategy that continue to surface when *Sunni* and *Shi'ah* groups each wage militant *jihad* on their own terms.[155] He makes the case that *Shi'ah* terrorism emanates from the policy objectives of the state of Iran and is executed as a campaign under the leadership of affiliates such as Hezbollah and the Islamic Jihad Organization. This differs in form and substance from *Sunni* terrorism, which Lynch describes as being motivated by a "theologically-driven . . . grandiose, ideological framework," that is executed as a wave.[156]

Samuel Helfont would not disagree with Lynch's thesis as far as it goes, but would add significantly to it. Helfont argues that if the task is "to assess the loyalties or predict the actions of various regional actors," then at least in the Middle East the dividing line in Islam lies *within* traditionalist *Sunni* Islam, with groups siding either with Wahhabism or with the Muslim Brotherhood.[157] As evidence, he points out that in both the 2006 Israeli-Hezbollah conflict in Lebanon, and in the 2008 Israeli-Hamas conflict in Gaza, regional politics did not divide along *Sunni-Shi'i* lines. Instead:

> . . . *Shias* from Hezbollah and Iran sided with *Sunni* Islamists from Hamas and other Muslim Brotherhood associated organizations. On the other side of the regional divide were *Sunni* Arab Nationalists, traditional *Sunni* monarchs, and *Sunni* Islamists with Wahhabist tendencies.[158]

For Helfont, these represent the enduring alignments of Middle East Islamic power.

Helfont shows that these two streams of *Sunni* Islam differ greatly today. Wahhabism and their affiliated groups, such as al-Qaeda, hold to radical traditionalist Islam.[159] They are motivated chiefly by theology, desiring to purify Islamic faith and practice by restoring radical traditionalist concepts of *Shari'ah*. Toward that end, radical Wahhabist organizations have endorsed *jihad* as offensive warfare against both the West and those Muslims deemed to be impure or corrupt.[160]

By way of contrast, Helfont characterizes Muslim Brotherhood organizations as chiefly political.[161] Willing to work with *Shi'i* and even non-Islamic groups if necessary, Muslim Brotherhood organizations seek to consolidate adequate power locally and regionally to build modern political systems that respect human rights while retaining an Islamic identity. Falling far short of the theological commitments of radical and even conservative Islam, the neotraditionalist Muslim Brotherhood is dedicated to political reform, concerned with western perception, and committed to building viable, modern Islamic states.

Just how different the Brotherhood can be from Wahhabism is shown in their approaches to *jihad*.[162] Given justifiable circumstances, the Brotherhood will employ any tactic of terrorist *jihad* from suicide bombings to using children as human shields, but only so long as the tactic may be construed as defensive. Their concerns for western perception and political settlement remain high. Wahhabists will also employ any terrorist tactic, but are willing to include *jihad* as offensive warfare because they see their warfare as divinely ordained. Not surprisingly, they accuse the Brotherhood of abandoning religious purity for political compromise. For the Brotherhood's part, they decry what they consider to be the Wahhabists' needless offenses against the West and their archaic and unworkable conceptions of the Islamic state. The strategic tension between Wahhabism and the Muslim Brotherhood is yet further magnified by Iran's drive for regional hegemony.[163]

In short, the need for nuance in understanding the Islamic world has never been greater. National security policy needs to address overlapping and competing alignments grounded in six Islamic positions, accounting for the division between traditionalist and reformed Islam, divisions within traditionalist Islam, the division within *Sunni* Islam between Wahhabism and the Brotherhood, Iran's drive for regional hegemony, and the power of other national and transnational Islamic organizations.[164]

Demographic Surveys.

Having examined a variety of Islamic positions, can we find demographic surveys which shed light on how various Muslims view the relationship of Islam to politics, the rule of *Shari'ah*, and the use of violent *jihad* and terrorist tactics? There have been relatively few scientific studies on the demographics of those who support radical Islam or terrorism.[165] John Esposito and Dali Mogahed have published their views based on certain polling data, but did not include the data.[166] The Pew Research Center's surveys provide arguably the most dependable, comprehensive data; their initial applicable survey is the December 4, 2002, report of the Pew Global Attitudes Project Report.[167]

Christine Fair and Bryan Shepherd have conducted rigorous analysis of the demographic variables represented in the 2002 Pew Report, yielding insights into Muslims who support terrorist tactics. Among the conclusions reached in their research are the following: (1) those who believe that Islam is under threat are much more likely to support terrorism, (2) those who believe that religious leaders should play a larger role in politics are substantially more likely to support terrorism, and (3) those who have a lower socioeconomic status are less likely to support terrorist acts.[168]

Below, I focus on data from the July 14, 2005, updated report of the Pew Global Attitudes Project Report and the 2007 Pew Research Study, *Muslim Americans: Middle Class and Mostly Mainstream*.[169] I have selected data that focuses on three areas: (1) the importance of Islam for Muslim identity and political life (Tables 2, 3, and 4); (2) the Muslim perception of the meaning, and associated threats, of Islamic extremism (Tables 5 and 6);[170] and (3) the level of support of Muslims for terrorist actions (Tables 7, 8, and 9).[171] Values in the tables represent the percentage of responders for each specific answer to a survey question.

The 2005 Pew Report establishes the primary importance of Islam for Muslim identity and political life. When Muslims were asked how they viewed themselves—as either a citizen or resident of their country first, or as a Muslim first—respondents generally answered that they were Muslims first. See Table 2.[172]

Country	Muslim First	Person of Country First	Both Identities Equal/VR*	DK/RA**
Turkey	43	29	27	1=100
Pakistan	79	7	13	1=100
Lebanon	30	30	39	1=100
Jordan	63	23	13	0=99
Morocco	70	7	23	0=100
Indonesia	39	35	26	0=100

*VR = "Voluntary response to the question." (here and in following tables).

** DK/RA = "Don't know, or refused to answer question" (here and in following tables).

**Table 2. Self Identity of Muslim or Citizen
(Muslim Respondents Only).**

This predominant religious identity carries over into the perceived role of Islam in political life. See Table 3.[173] When asked how much of a role they thought Islam played in the political life of their country, most Muslims saw Islam playing a very large or fairly large role. Comparing the 2002 data to the 2005 data does not suggest an overall trend.

Country (Year of Data)	Very Large Role	Fairly Large Role	Fairly Small Role	Very Small Role	DK/RA
Turkey 2005	30	32	16	14	8=100
Turkey 2002	21	25	19	24	11=100
Pakistan 2005	38	24	12	9	17=100
Pakistan 2002	35	21	11	16	17=100
Lebanon 2005	22	32	35	5	6=100
Lebanon 2002	33	38	15	8	6=100
Jordan 2005	10	20	49	19	2=100
Jordan 2002	25	25	27	22	0=99
Morocco 2005	57	18	9	9	7=100
Indonesia 2005	33	52	11	2	2=100
Indonesia 2002	39	47	10	2	2=100

**Table 3. Role of Islam in Political Life
(2002 data corrected March 3, 2007).**

Although no overall trend may exist between the 2002 to the 2005 data in Table 3, Muslims themselves believe that the religion of Islam is playing a generally greater or equal role in their countries compared to a few years ago. See Table 4.[174]

	Greater Role	Lesser Role	No Change/VR	DK/RA
Turkey	47	32	14	7=100
Pakistan	48	23	12	16=99
Lebanon	35	17	25	23=100
Jordan	18	43	38	1=100
Morocco	57	28	4	11=100
Indonesia	73	15	9	2=99

Table 4. Greater or Lesser Role of Islam in Politics Compared to a Few Years Ago.

The 2005 Pew Report shows the difficulty in trying to define Muslim extremism. The survey asked Muslims to define what Islamic extremism means to them by choosing between two options: (1) advocating the legal imposition of strict *Shari'ah* on all Muslims, or (2) using violence to get rid of non-Muslim influences in their country. See Table 5.[175] Because the two options are both marks of the position of traditionalist Islam, adding the two together would likely yield the minimum number of traditionalist Muslims in each country. Strict *Shari'ah* and the potential use of militant *jihad* are marks of the position of traditionalist Islam.

Country	Impose Strict Shari'ah on All Muslims	Use Violence to Remove All Non-Muslim Influences	DK/RA
Turkey	48	16	36=100
Pakistan	36	22	42=100
Lebanon	35	46	19=100
Jordan	36	60	4=100
Morocco	20	53	27=100
Indonesia	50	30	20=100

Table 5. What Islamic Extremism Means.

After noting support for possible meanings of Islamic extremism, the 2005 Pew Report turns to the more significant question of the nature of the perceived threats posed by Islamic extremism. Individuals were asked what concerned them most about Islamic extremism in their own country. Options included: "It is violent," "It will lead to people having fewer personal freedoms and choices," "It will divide the country," and "It will set back economic development." See Table 6.[176]

Country	Is Violent	Leads to Fewer Freedoms	Divides the Country	Sets Back Development	None/VR	DK/RA
Turkey	25	28	29	9	2	6=99
Pakistan	17	15	24	28	5	12=101
Lebanon	24	36	29	9	3	1=102
Jordan	21	37	26	15	1	0=100
Morocco	37	20	24	14	1	4=100
Indonesia	41	20	19	15	2	3=100

Table 6. Perceived Threats of Islamic Extremism in One's Country.

It is interesting that in Table 6 the mean scores for violence (27.5), loss of freedom (26.0), and division of country (25.2) are so close to each other. In these Islamic countries, the concern over violent Islamic extremism — or, more precisely, violence from Islamic traditionalism and terrorism — is essentially as intense as the concern over having fewer personal freedoms or having a country with greater divisions as a result of Islamic extremism. This suggests a level of acceptance regarding violence and terrorism within Islamic societies that is fundamentally higher than is usually found in Western societies, at least by comparison with the other accompanying threats.

Additional data from the 2007 Pew Study survey seems to bear this out. Individuals were posed the following question, with responses summarized in Table 7:

> Some people think that suicide bombing and other forms of violence against civilian targets are justified in order to defend Islam from its enemies. Other people believe that, no matter what the reason, this kind of violence is never justified. Do you personally feel that this kind of violence is often justified to defend Islam, sometimes justified, rarely justified, or never justified?[177]

Justified	USA*	Muslims in Europe April 2006 Data				Muslims only in Muslim Countries April 2006 Data					
		Britain	France	Germany	Spain	Egypt	Turkey	Indonesia	Pakistan	Jordan	Nigeria
Often	1	3	6	1	6	8	3	2	7	5	8
Sometimes	7	12	10	6	10	20	14	8	7	24	38
Rarely	5	9	19	6	9	25	9	18	8	28	23
Never	78	70	64	83	69	45	61	71	69	43	28
DK/RA	9	6	1	3	7	3	14	1	8	0	3
Total	100	100	100	99	101	101	101	100	99	100	100

* = USA Muslim respondent only data from May 2007.

**Table 7. How Often Terrorist Acts against Civilians Justified
(Muslim respondents only).**

Based on Table 7 data, the number of Muslims who view terrorist acts against civilians as justified "often" or "sometimes" is quite high, ranging to over 20 percent in Egypt and Jordan, and over 40 percent in Nigeria.[178] To grasp the full extent of the acceptance of terrorist acts among Muslims surveyed, one must add all three categories of those who see terrorism as ever justified — often, sometimes, and rarely. See Table 8.

Aggregated Data		Muslims in Europe April 2006 Data				Muslims only in Muslim Countries April 2006 Data					
Justified	USA*	Britain	France	Germany	Spain	Egypt	Turkey	Indonesia	Pakistan	Jordan	Nigeria
Ever **	13	24	35	13	25	53	26	28	22	57	69
Never	78	70	64	83	69	45	61	71	69	43	28
DK/RA	9	6	1	3	7	3	14	1	8	0	3
Total	100	100	100	99	101	101	101	100	99	100	100

* = USA Muslim respondent only data from May 2007.
** = Aggregated data from respondents, the sum of all responses that said that terrorist acts can ever be justified — often, sometimes, and rarely.

**Table 8. How Often Terrorist Acts against Civilians Justified
(Muslim respondents only).**

For example, data from Table 8 show that in the United States 13 percent of all Muslims believe that some terrorist acts against civilians can be justified. If one extrapolates this sample to the 2007 Pew Study estimate of 2.35 million Muslims in America, this could translate into as many as 300,000 American Muslims who find certain terrorist acts justified.[179] By comparison, the percentages of Muslims in Egypt, Jordan, and Nigeria who responded that certain acts of terror can be justified exceeded 50 percent.

This data does not appear to be anomalous. The 2005 Pew Report followed the above general question about Muslim perception of terrorist acts being justified with a specific question about the use of suicide bombing against Americans and other Westerners in Iraq: Were such terrorist actions justifiable or not? See Table 9.[180]

Country	Justifiable	Not Justifiable	DK/RA
Turkey	24	62	14=100
Pakistan	29	56	15=100
Lebanon	49	43	10=100
Jordan	49	43	8=100
Morocco	56	40	4=100
Indonesia	26	67	7=100

Table 9. Are Suicide Bombings against Americans and Westerners in Iraq Justifiable?

The approximately one-quarter to one-half of surveyed Muslims who responded that terrorist acts in Iraq against Americans and other Westerners were justifiable corresponds roughly to the data in Table 8 for Muslims within Muslim countries and their rates of ever finding terrorist acts justified. By country, there is apparant agreement between these data sets.

We cannot say how many of these Muslims who justify terrorist acts would self-identify with radical, conservative, or neotraditionalist Islamic positions, all of which leave open the possibility of legitimate, violent *jihad*. However, it is important to note that the survey question used to gather the data for Tables 7 and 8 specifically asked about violence being justified "to defend Islam." This is the language of *jihad* and, because of this, we may reasonably infer that Muslim respondents' personal acceptance of violent *jihad* was reflected in their rates of finding acts of terror justified.

III. RELIGION AS PARADIGM IN NATIONAL SECURITY POLICY

We have seen that religion will continue to play a powerful role in influencing matters of conflict and security, and that nuance will be needed to address the varying positions within Islam. Alternative paradigms for integrating religion within national security policy are now considered, beginning with the national security policy of President George W. Bush (2001-09).

Religion in the National Security Policy of President George W. Bush.

Because President Bush was quite open about his religious faith, it is important to briefly consider the relationship of his faith to his national security policy. President Bush's evangelical Christian faith undoubtedly provided motivation and guidance for him in his private and public life.[181] His faith also affected his construal of the adversary in the Global War on Terrorism (GWOT).[182] That said, it appears President Bush set policy based on his view of universal values, not his religion. For example, he saw freedom and human kindness as universal values created by God — not by the United States — for the benefit of all.[183] A critical component of that freedom was religious freedom. Because of this, it made sense to President Bush to use national security policy to encourage growth of religious freedom in problematic societies, irrespective of whether their religion was fundamentally different from his own.[184]

This view of religion as an expression of the universal value of freedom was reflected in President Bush's 2002 National Security Strategy (NSS) and again in his NSS 2006.[185] These two documents will be used as representative of his national security policy.

NSS 2002 was a wartime document released just 1 year after 9/11. It framed the GWOT as a war in defense of freedom and human dignity. The broader purpose of NSS 2002 — "to create a balance of power that favors human freedom" — aligned with its foundational assumption that "freedom is the non-negotiable demand of human dignity; the birthright of every person — in every civilization."[186]

Toward the end of defending freedom within the homeland and abroad, NSS 2002 expressed eight strategic imperatives. The first, and arguably primary, imperative focused on growing freedom by championing the non-negotiable components of a free society which included "freedom of worship" and "religious . . . tolerance."[187] Moreover, NSS 2002 articulated policy ways to achieve these freedoms: Speak out clearly about violations of these freedoms, use foreign aid to support those who struggle nonviolently for these freedoms, develop these freedoms through bilateral relations, and "take special efforts to promote freedom of religion and conscience and defend it from encroachment by repressive governments."[188] If my reading of NSS 2002 is correct, this promotion of religious freedom was also intended to buttress the "war of ideas" against international terrorism. By supporting moderate Muslim governments in their efforts to build freer and more robust societies, the United States would make it harder for terrorists to plant their violent ideologies.[189]

NSS 2006 similarly emphasized freedom as a universal desire, but it went further by elevating religious freedom to the status of "First Freedom":

> Against a terrorist enemy that is defined by religious intolerance, we defend the First Freedom: the right of people to believe and worship according to the dictates of their own conscience, free from the coercion of the state, the coercion of the majority, or the coercion of a minority that wants to dictate what others must believe.[190]

NSS 2006 also offered additional policy ways to promote freedom of religion.[191]

Beyond these incremental changes, NSS 2006 did advance a substantive addition to the role of religion in national security policy. It offered a strategic message that Islam was a "proud religion," that was being "twisted and made to serve an evil end."[192] It characterized terrorists as turning the concept of *jihad* into a "call for murder," eliminating any religious freedom to disagree, even among Muslims.[193] To meet this threat, NSS 2006 offered both long-term and short-term strategies.[194]

Religion in the National Security Policy of President Barack Obama.

Less than 1 month after his inauguration in January 2009, during remarks at the first National Prayer Breakfast of his administration, President Obama grounded his understanding of the role of religion in world affairs in his personal faith experience.[195] Connected to a religiously diverse family and raised by a mother skeptical of organized religion, he came to view his mother as the most spiritual person he had ever known. She taught him "to love, and to understand, and to do unto others as I would want done."[196] This understanding later became decisive for his own faith, which germinated in the context of community organizing in Chicago:

> I didn't become a Christian until many years later, when I moved to the South Side of Chicago after college. It happened not because of indoctrination or a sudden revelation, but because I spent month after month working with church folks who simply wanted to help neighbors who were down on their luck—no matter what they looked like, or where they came from, or who they prayed to.[197]

This personal faith perspective has led President Obama to articulate a positive view of religion as a force for unity. For him, belief systems may vary, but all Christians, Jews, Muslims, Buddhists, Hindus, Confucians, and secular humanists stand united: "There is one law that binds all great religions together. . . . the Golden Rule—the call to love one another; to understand one another; to treat with dignity and respect those with whom we share a brief moment on this Earth."[198] Based on this understanding of the essential nature of religion, President Obama has rejected as false any religion that would preach hate or condone the taking of innocent life.[199]

This view of religion as a force for unity is reflected in President Obama's national security policy. To examine this view, I have used as sources the following major speeches which bear on the role of religion in his national security policy—President Obama's January 20, 2009, Inaugural Address in Washington, DC (henceforth, Inaugural Address); his April 6, 2009, remarks to the Turkish Parliament in Ankara, Turkey (henceforth, Ankara); his June 4, 2009, *On a New Beginning* speech at Cairo University, Cairo, Egypt (henceforth, Cairo); his July 11, 2009, *New Moment of Promise* speech to the Ghanaian Parliament in Accra, Ghana (henceforth, Accra); his November 10, 2009 remarks at the memorial service at Fort Hood, TX (henceforth, Fort Hood); and his December 1, 2009, *On the Way Forward in Afghanistan and Pakistan* speech at West Point, NY (henceforth, West Point).[200]

In his Inaugural Address, President Obama announced the beginning of a new policy of rapprochement with the Muslim world based on "mutual interest and mutual respect." In Ankara, he began to unfold this policy by identifying three main objectives bearing on religion. The United States would work with the Muslim world to (1) "[roll] back violent ideologies that people of all faiths reject"; (2) listen respectfully, conquer misunderstandings, and seek common ground; and (3) "convey our deep appreciation for the Islamic faith."[201] Here President Obama began to edge past President Bush's NSS 2006 position by calling on the United States to praise the religion of Islam and by implying that Muslim terrorists were not true Muslims. In a side note, President Obama also encouraged diversity of religious expression as important for building strong and vibrant societies.[202]

In Cairo, President Obama retained his three-fold emphases from Ankara, but expanded them in his bid to make "a new beginning" with Islam. Going beyond the language of common interests with the Muslim world, President Obama spoke of a "partnership between America and Islam [that] must be based on what Islam is, not what it isn't. And I consider it part of my responsibility as President of the United States to fight against negative stereotypes of Islam wherever they appear." Toward that end, the President argued that the actions of terrorists placed them outside the religion of Islam.[203] Moreover, he maintained that Islam participated in a fundamental unity with all religions: "There's one rule that lies at the heart of every religion—that we do unto others as we would have them do unto us. . . . It's a faith in other people, and it's what brought me here today." Based on this concept of shared faith, the President challenged his Muslim audience: "We have the power to make the world we seek, but only if we have the courage to make a new beginning."[204] Retaining his previous side note, the President also encouraged his audience to embrace religious diversity to enable all people to live together.

At Accra, Fort Hood, and West Point, President Obama continued to portray religion as a force for unity in matters of national security. At Accra, President Obama rejected as false any religion that would define itself over against another faith: "Defining oneself in opposition to someone . . . who worships a different prophet, has no place in the 21st century. . . . We are all God's children."[205] At Fort Hood, during the memorial service following the shooting that left 13 dead and 30 injured, the President reasoned that all true religions were united against such acts of violence: "No faith justifies these murderous and craven acts; no just and loving God looks upon them with favor."[206] At West Point, President Obama judged al-Qaeda terrorists to be beyond the pale of true religion, having "distorted and defiled Islam, one of the world's great religions, to justify the slaughter of innocents." Returning to the language of mutual interests between America and the Muslim world, the President called for partnership in "breaking a cycle of conflict," and in "[isolating] those who kill innocents."[207]

Three Paradigms for the Role of Religion in National Security Policy.

Religion as Freedom. The role of religion in the national security of policy of President Bush suggests a paradigm of Religion as Freedom.[208] The narrative of this paradigm runs as follows: Freedom is a universal value. All people everywhere desire to live in free societies securely, with equal rights under the law. Chief among these rights is the freedom to choose one's religion and worship according to one's conscience. Current adversaries such as the Taliban and al-Qaeda wield power defined by religious intolerance, intending to establish repressive rule that would deny inhabitants their freedoms. To defeat these adversaries, the long-term solution requires working within the Muslim world to build and strengthen democratic institutions in order to protect the rule of law and individual freedoms, including the freedom of religion.[209]

This paradigm suggests certain national security policy options that leverage Religion as Freedom:

1. Support moderate Muslim governments and isolate radical Muslim terrorists to help build freer societies and to make it harder for terrorists to plant their violent ideologies of religious intolerance;

2. Champion religious freedom and speak out clearly against religious oppression;

3. Praise the actions of, and award foreign aid to, moderate Islamic governments that work to promote freedom of religion;

4. Build religious freedom through linkage with other policies across all elements of national power;

5. Work multilaterally to encourage Islamic governments to support freedom of religion and to discourage terrorists who repress such freedoms; and,

6. Show religious sensitivity.

Analysis of the paradigm of Religion as Freedom follows: The pros of this paradigm are that it resonates with the enduring American value of freedom; is fully transparent to the American public; enables a slightly nuanced understanding of various Islamic positions, distinguishing between those which support freedom of religion and those which do not; and takes the long view of growing peace in the Muslim world by growing institutions of freedom. The cons of this paradigm are that it emphasizes a western concept of freedom to choose and worship God over an Islamic concept to submit to God, omits any discussion of the decisive nature of Islamic unity,[210] fails to promote understanding of evolving alignments within traditionalist Islam,[211] and locks itself into a monolithic freedom framework for addressing the role of religion in future conflicts. These problems suggest that this paradigm will not find traction in the Muslim world, at least in the short run.

Religion as Unity. The role of religion in the national security policy of President Obama suggests a paradigm of Religion as Unity.[212] The narrative of this paradigm runs as follows: All religions are bound together by a universal moral law to love one another and to treat each other with dignity and respect. Religion is, in the final analysis, faith in humanity. Because of this, the religions of the world are a powerful force for unity if properly used to encourage people to work to understand each other and to resolve conflict. Any religion that preaches otherwise—propagating hate, violence, or opposition toward another religion—is no true religion, but only a fraud and defilement. Islam is a religion which embraces peace and rejects violence. Current adversaries such as the Taliban and al-Qaeda represent no religion, only hate and violence. To defeat these adversaries, the long-term solution requires forming an enduring partnership with the Muslim world, seeking opportunities to honor the Muslim faith, addressing mutual misunderstandings, and locating and pursuing mutual interests.

This paradigm suggests certain national security policy options that leverage Religion as Unity:

1. Enter into dialog with all Muslim governments in order to show honor to Islam, resolve mutual misunderstandings, pursue mutual interests, and especially to isolate violent terrorists.

2. Integrate the strategic communication that all true religions are a powerful force for unity through their common commitment to love humanity, spread peace, and reject violence;

3. Champion Islam as a religion of peace, and fight negative stereotypes;

4. Praise the actions of, and award foreign aid to, moderate Muslim governments which work to resolve disagreements through dialog and non-violent means;

5. Work multilaterally to encourage Islamic governments to marginalize violent ideologies and enact policies that show dignity and respect to people of all faiths; and,

6. Show religious sensitivity.

Analysis of the paradigm of Religion as Unity follows: The pros of this paradigm are that it resonates with many Muslims through its praise of Islam, it undercuts certain terrorist recruitment arguments which vilify the West, it leverages religion as a force for unity, it takes an immediate view of growing peace in the Muslim world through open dialog with all Muslim governments, and it promotes some understanding of evolving alignments within traditionalist Islam through open dialog. The cons of this paradigm are that it employs a concept of religious unity that assesses a moral equivalence between world religions, which traditionalist Muslims do not accept; generalizes Islam into a caricature of peace, failing to provide a nuanced understanding of varying Islamic faith positions or to address data that show support for terrorist tactics between 22 percent and 69 percent in certain Muslim countries;[213] appears to lack full transparency to Americans who are aware of rates of Muslim support for terrorism; omits any discussion of the decisive nature of Islamic unity;[214] and locks itself into a monolithic unity framework for addressing the role of religion in future conflicts. These problems suggest that this paradigm will run headlong into serious difficulties in the long run.

Religion as Ideology. The preceding discussion of the paradigms of Religion as Freedom and Religion as Unity shows how hard it is to locate an adequate framework for integrating religion into national security policy today. Each paradigm has its strengths and weaknesses, but neither rises to the level where its discussion of religion contributes robustly to the promotion of national security.

We must certainly value the strengths of these paradigms. Each paradigm brings an important truth to the table. We should understand freedom of religion as a necessary component of free and robust societies, and work to plant and nourish that freedom. It is also true that religions often share a moral commitment to care for one's neighbor, and that cooperative ventures to meet human needs can build human trust. Each paradigm rightly encourages respect for religious expression and commitment.

That said, we must also account for the weaknesses of these paradigms. Taking a step back and looking at the entire policy formulation process, the reason for the weaknesses becomes clear. Although each paradigm brings an important perspective to the table, each does so apart from a prior assessment of Islamic power within the strategic environment. It is all well and good to begin with the enduring values of the United States (as the Religion as Freedom paradigm does), or liberal democratic values (as the Religion as Unity paradigm does), and then to frame national interests in terms of those values. However, policy rests not only on national interests, but also on a grand strategy and strategic vision that comprehends strategic power and threat. Operationally, the adversary always gets a vote. To frame the adversary in terms of our enduring national values or liberal democratic values—which is essentially what each of these two paradigms does—will ensure that our strategic vision and policy, although partially correct, are fundamentally flawed. The adversary must be known in terms of *his* values, *his* center of gravity, and *his* objectives. Effective policy rests on the creative interplay of values which beget our national interests, with our strategic vision which comprehends the nature of the power of an adversary.

This means that there can be no adequate determination of the role of religion in national security policy apart from a logically prior and accurate assessment of an adversary and his power. In the case of our current adversaries, this means that we must first understand radical Muslims and terrorists by way of *their* values, *their* center of gravity, and *their* objectives. To the extent that these are based in religion, we must understand their view of, and participation in, Islam as power. Only then can policymakers bring our values-generated interests to bear on the adversary's power as it actually exists.

This suggests a new paradigm for the role of religion in national security policy. If, at the level of grand strategy and strategic vision, religion matters as a source of power, then at the level of policy religion matters as a source of behavior. Religion motivates, enables, and directs behavior, which can have consequences for national security. In this sense, we are not discussing religion in its capacity as divine path, but religion in its capacity as ideology, i.e., as a moral framework of ideas that drives actions, values, and objectives. This is what I mean by the paradigm of Religion as Ideology.

This paradigm is particularly important because the U.S. Government is religion-neutral.[215] There is no place in U.S. national security policy for religion in the capacity of advocate for one faith or judge of another, but only for religion in its capacity as empowerment of human behavior. The focus must not be on belief, but on behavior. Such empowered behavior must be in view as national security policy frames its options to influence behavior toward the ends of our grand strategy in support of our national interests. This is especially critical because religious behavior frequently reflects the fullness of human aspiration in light of the breadth and depth of the human condition.

Section II of this paper attempted to provide the underpinnings of an estimate for a grand strategy and strategic vision that comprehends Islam as power. The paradigm of Religion as Ideology would argue the necessity of contextualizing this understanding of Islam as power before generating related national security policy options. First, distinguish Islamic actors at the transnational, national, regional, and local levels by their behaviors. Identify their actions which demonstrate their understanding of *jihad*, their concept of universalizing Islam, their position relative to alignments within traditionalist Islam, and their support of terrorist violence. Second, for analytical purposes, aggregate those actors who demonstrate similar actions, values, and objectives. Only then, formulate policy options in light of our values-generated interests.

Examples of policy options might include:

1. Integrate the strategic communication that the United States is committed to enhanced freedom, peace, and prosperity for its Muslim friends, but will oppose all those who use violence to achieve their political ends.

2. Informed by the above critical distinctions regarding Islam as power, issue statements that articulate ideological differences between Islamic actors in terms of behaviors and objectives, taking care to neither praise nor judge the religion of Islam. In these statements, identify positive actions such as participating in peaceful dialog and consensus building, committing publicly to peaceful coexistence with those of different faiths, protecting broader freedoms, honoring the value of every human life, showing respect for religious diversity, and meet critical human needs. Also identify negative actions such as violence and repression against innocents, against women, and against those of other faiths; support for terrorism; and destruction of infrastructure.

3. Enact a diversified policy of engagement with a continuum of rewards and support for actors with positive behavior, and consequences for actors with negative behav-

ior. Use this diversified policy to move Islamic groups and governments incrementally toward the positive end of the spectrum.

4. Work multilaterally wherever possible to support moderate Muslim governments and isolate radical Muslim terrorists by revealing the full costs of their actions.

5. Use available elements of national power, both soft and hard, to support our national interests and the mutual interests we hold with the Muslim world.

6. Synchronize policy actions across the interagency.

7. Show religious sensitivity.

8. Encourage respect for religious commitments.

The advantages of the paradigm of Religion as Ideology are numerous. First, this paradigm is based on a strategic vision that comprehends the power of Islam understood in terms of varying concepts of universalizing Islam, different forms of *jihad*, evolving alignments within traditionalist Islam, and various levels of support for terrorist violence. Second, it promotes a more nuanced understanding of different Islamic groups based on their behavior. Third, it allows a diversified continuum of carrot-and-stick responses based on the relative behaviors of actors. Fourth, it brings the fullness of American values to bear through articulated national interests vis-à-vis national security issues, without the limitations inherent in monolithic paradigms such as Religion as Freedom, or Religion as Unity. Fifth, it should appeal to moderate Muslim governments as the United States works multilaterally to pursue mutual interests and isolate terrorists. Sixth, it conforms to the traditions of the religiously neutral U.S. Government, neither advocating for nor detracting for any religion, but only focusing on behaviors in light of national security concerns. Finally, the paradigm of Religion as Ideology should appeal to the American public as fully transparent.

There are, nonetheless, at least two risks associated with implementing this paradigm. First, changing from the paradigm of Religion as Unity to the paradigm of Religion as Ideology might appear to some western and moderate Islamic audiences to signal a new, negative orientation toward Islam. Second, terrorist recruiters might seize on the changed rhetoric of a United States which is no longer praising Islam as yet further justification for fighting the West.

IV. THE WAY AHEAD

Section I of this paper has shown that religion matters and will continue to matter in national security challenges for the foreseeable future. Toffler, Fukuyama, Huntington, and Kaplan may point to different root causes of future conflict, but all emphasize religion as a critical component in policy that would address those challenges. This is all the more true because religion frequently reflects the fullness of human aspiration against the sobering reality of the human condition.

The analysis of the power of Islam provided in Section II revealed an Islam that is far from monolithic. Islam today is manifested in many forms, reflecting multiple perspectives on how the faith is to achieve its universalization, on what *jihad* means, and on when, if ever, terrorist tactics are justifiable in defense of Islam. Traditionalist conceptions of Islam maintain the continuing applicability of *Shari'ah* as state law, and the potentiality for *jihad* as warfare, with an average of over 20 percent of Muslims in

Muslim-majority nations finding terrorist acts at times to be justifiable in defense of Islam. Liberal and post-modern reformists, on the other hand, generally condemn violent *jihad* and seek peaceful relations with the West. An accurate assessment of Islam as power will inform the grand strategy and strategic vision on which effective national security policy rests.

A review of the national security policies of President George W. Bush and President Barack Obama in Section III has demonstrated the incredible difficulty of bringing religion to bear within national security policy. Weighing the alternative paradigms of Religion as Freedom, Religion as Unity, and Religion as Ideology, I have suggested that the last paradigm offers the greatest utility. It calls for a strategic vision that comprehends the power of Islam, it enables a nuanced understanding of Islamic groups based on their behavior, it facilitates a diversified continuum of policy rewards and consequences based on that behavior, and it refrains from violating the American tradition of the federal government neither advocating for nor judging a religion.

Certain practical matters will need to be addressed if religion is to gain currency within national security policy. If we move closer to the paradigm of Religion as Ideology, it will be important to head off any erroneous public perception that the United States is shifting to a negative strategy toward Islam. U.S. officials will need to state emphatically that America has no policy for or against any religion, that we promote full freedom of worship, and that we seek partnership based on mutual interests and mutual respect with people of all religions. Actions will need to follow these words. The United States will need to reach out with renewed vigor through diplomatic summits and multilateral engagements with the Muslim world to build consensus wherever possible. Certainly, this would include partnership in the continued defense and support of peaceful Islamic governments against terrorist violence.

To support a more robust role of religion in national security policy, U.S. combatant commands should consider ways to include religion in all campaign design and planning. Campaign design activities include framing and reframing the operational environment, problem, and operational approach. Designing with religion in mind will help combatant commanders better understand their actual environment, grasp the deep roots of complex problems, and create opportunities to provide enduring solutions.

Campaign planning should also include vigorous consideration of religion. In current overseas contingency operations, religion contributes directly to stakeholder identity, power, strategic alignment, and operational outcome. To strengthen planning, one option would be to integrate religion as a phased line of effort (LOE) in addition to current LOEs defined by political, military, economic, social, infrastructure, and informational systems.[216] This would raise religion's operational significance, but might risk reducing its human significance if religion were to become merely a manipulated element of power. Another option would be to add religion as a supporting objective under both the political and social LOEs. This would again raise religion's operational significance, but might additionally elucidate its human significance within political and social systems. Religion must be understood as a power directing, guiding, and living through the behavioral choices of its adherents across formal and informal political, social, and cultural systems.

An issue of supreme importance will involve calculating the strategic room needed for various conceptions of achieving the universalization of Islam. As argued in Section II, the critical issue for Islam today is determining how the faith will achieve its final vision of unity. Various positions within Islam answer this question differently—radical Muslims through the mechanism of militant *jihad*; conservative Muslims through the vision of a united *ummah* living under *Shari'ah*; neotraditionalist Muslims through an updated integration of Islamic tradition within their respective societies; reformed Muslims through a determination and application of enduring Islamic principles to enable Muslim life in modern societies; and secular-state Muslims through a private and community practice of *Shari'ah* which excludes the power relations of government. In all cases, policymakers will need to understand the conceptions of universalization to which various Islamic positions aspire. Even more, policymakers will need to determine how much active support or passive space U.S. national interests can afford or allow toward the fulfillment of those aspirations. Knowing the parameters could amount to a national security imperative.

Finally, that religion will continue to matter, and matter a lot, in U.S. national security challenges may be a bitter pill for secularist Western liberals to swallow. Certain political advisers, academics, and senior leaders of the professions of arms may find it difficult to believe that many 21st-century people are still motivated by religion, and that some are even willing to fight and die for their beliefs. Their incredulity is easy to document. National security policy statements, academic texts on cultural frameworks, and even military manuals on counterinsurgency doctrine can discuss their subject matter without examining religion as a power which motivates human behavior. I encourage all to rethink their assumptions and reengage in these critical arenas.

ENDNOTES

1. I wish to express my deep gratitude for the contributions of Dr. Tami Davis Biddle. Her global perspective, national security insights, and sensitivity to perceptions over religious issues provided critical context and caution as I wrote this monograph. Dr Biddle is Professor of National Security Strategy and Military History at the U.S. Army War College, Carlisle, Pannsylvania.

National security policy rightly addresses both internal and external threats that impact the enduring beliefs, ethics, and values; the national interests; and the grand strategy of the nation state. This monograph largely bypasses discussion of internal threats to focus on external threats and the role of religion in visualizing and meeting those threats.

2. Sun Tzu, *The Art of War*, Samuel B. Griffith, trans., London, United Kingdom (UK): Oxford University Press, Oxford Paperbacks, 1971, p. 84.

3. Carl von Clausewitz, *On War*, Michael and Peter Paret, eds. and trans., Princeton, NJ: Princeton University Press, 1976, p. 89. Von Clausewitz conceives of war at its most basic level as "primordial violence, hatred, and enmity." To empower such violent conflict, "the passions that are to be kindled in war must already be inherent in the people." Why would one omit religion as a constitutive power within a society, especially as that power comes into play in the calculus of war?

4. The Judeo-Christian heritage participated in the West's just war tradition, which grounds war in the civil realm's responsibility to prevent harm to innocents and punish evil doers in the cause of justice.

Islam possesses its own just war tradition which grounds war historically and theologically in the necessity of the struggle to defend and spread the faith. See the monumental volume, Andrew G. Bostom, ed., *The Legacy of Jihad: Islamic Holy War and the Fate of Non-Muslims*, with a foreward by Ibn Warraq. Amherst, NY: Prometheus Books, 2005. Bostom provides voluminous primary source materials translated for the English reader. For a helpful discussion of Islamic conceptions of *jus ad bellum* and *jus in bello*, see *The Islamic Law of Nations: Shaybani's Siyar*, trans. and Introduction by Majid Khadduri, Baltimore, MD: John Hopkins Press, 1966.

5. Adolf Köberle, *The Quest for Holiness*, John C. Mattes, trans., from the 3d German Ed., Evansville, IN: Ballast Press, 1999. In his sweeping analysis, Köberle examines world religions against the frameworks of moralism, mysticism, and speculation, and their engines of will, spirit, and thought. He tracks the inevitable futility of theological synergism, which he demonstrates can finally be overcome only by a robust divine monergism which, by the declaration of acceptance and the gift of the Spirit in Christ, enables human fulfillment and sanctification. Köberle was a confessional Lutheran scholar and professor at the University of Basel.

6. *Ibid.*, p. 1. Latin: "Grant us peace."

7. Federal pronouncements that would promote or proclaim the comparative value of a religion could, on the one hand, violate the First Amendment of the U.S. Constitution for internal audiences, and on the other, be inappropriate and even counterproductive for foreign audiences.

8. The date of 9/11 is commonly used to mark the start of persistent conflict for the United States. Equally significant is that this persistent conflict has been oriented against an adversary who defines himself chiefly in terms of religion vis-à-vis America and the West. How America and the West define the adversary is another matter. The third section of this monograph focuses on the post-9/11 timeframe through an examination of the national security policies of President George W. Bush and President Barack Obama.

9. By historiographers, I mean those who write on history as a phenomenon and propose a paradigmatic view of history. This does not mean that the four authors herein surveyed consider themselves, or are, primarily historiographers. Indeed, Francis Fukuyama and Samuel Huntington have used historiography as a tool for their major discipline of political science.
I am especially indebted to Dr Adam Francisco for his insight that a serious discussion today on the role of religion in national security policy requires handling the issues raised in Francis Fukuyama's and Samuel Huntington's disparate treatments of religions connection to the world of human conflict. This insight helped determine the structure of this monograph. Dr. Francisco is Associate Professor of history at Concordia University Irvine, Irvine, California.

10. In only a very limited sense dows Section II of this monograph—by way of an historical review of Islam—provide a window to past connections of religion to national security policy.

11. Alvin Toffler, *The Third Wave*, New York: William Morrow and Company, Inc., 1980. Francis Fukuyama, *The End of History and the Last Man*, New York: Free Press, 1992. Fukuyama's book represents a substantial development beyond his initial investigation published as "The End of History?" *The National Interest*, Vol. 16, Summer 1989, pp. 3-18. Samuel P. Huntington, *The Clash of Civilizations and the Remaking of World Order*, New York: Simon & Schuster, 1996. This book develops in detail, and asserts the validity of, the hypothesis that Huntington initially published in question form, "The Clash of Civilizations?" *Foreign Affairs*, Vol. 72, No. 3, Summer 1993, pp. 22-49. Robert D. Kaplan, *The Coming Anarchy: Shattering the Dreams of the Post Cold War*, New York: Random House, 2000. Chap. 1, "The Coming Anarchy," was first published in the February 1994 edition of *The Atlantic Monthly*.

12. Alvin Toffler, an American futurist, has written on patterns of societal change, to include revolutions in the fields of technology, communication, and business. For further background on Toffler and his futurist views, see Peter Schwartz, "Shock Wave (Anti) Warrior," *Wired* 1.05, November 1993, available from *www.wired.com/wired/archive/1.05/toffler.html*.

13. Toffler, p. 25.

14. *Ibid.*

15. *Ibid.*, chaps. 11-23, pp. 143-365.

16. *Ibid.*, p. 21.

17. In discussing First and Second Wave confluence, Toffler emphasizes battles internal to a society, although he also touches on external violence. At p. 39:

As the Second Wave moved across various societies it touched off a bloody, protracted war between the defenders of the agricultural past and the partisans of the industrial future. The forces of First and Second Wave collided head-on, brushing aside, often decimating, the "primitive" peoples encountered along the way.

For further discussion, see chap. 2, "The Architecture of Civilization," pp. 37-52.

18. *Ibid.*, p. 453.

19. *Ibid.*, p. 134.

20. *Ibid.*, p. 375. Similarly, at p. 273: "Our religious views, like our tastes, are becoming less uniform and standardized."

21. *Ibid.*, p. 26.

22. *Ibid.*, p. 306.

23. *Ibid.*, pp. 390-392, quote at p. 392.

24. *Ibid.*, p. 435:

The first, heretical principle of Third Wave government is that of minority power. It holds that majority rule, the key legitimating principle of the Second Wave era, is increasingly obsolete. It is not majorities but minorities that count. And our political systems must increasingly reflect that fact.

25. *Ibid.*, p. 347. Toffler terms the long-term struggle in civilization between the Second and Third Waves "the coming super-struggle." Religion will continue as a source of traditional conflict, but, more significantly for Toffler, will also be absorbed as a critical component within the larger ideological super-struggle. See Toffler, pp. 25-34, 452-456.

26. Fukuyama has written broadly on state governance, political and economic development, social order, biotechnology, and the philosophy of history. He currently serves as professor at the Paul H. Nitze School of Advanced International Studies of Johns Hopkins University, Washington, DC. For further information, consult his biography posted at the website for the Paul H. Nitze School of Advanced International Studies, available from *www.sais-jhu.edu/faculty/ fukuyama/Biography.html.*

27. *Ibid.*, p. 55. For an overview of Fukuyama's argument, see his introductory chapter, "By Way of an Introduction," pp. xi-xxiii.

Fukuyama frequently uses the word "man" in its universal and generic sense, to denote in the concrete, individual case the fullness of humanity therein presented. In the discussion which follows, I retain Fukuyama's usage of "man." In related terminology, Fukuyama also speaks of the "last man," i.e., that man who is the final manifestation of human evolution, who no longer possesses the fullness of what previously had properly belonged to humanity.

28. See Fukuyama, Chap. 1, "Our Pessimism," pp. 3-12, in which he rejects the pessimism founded on 20th century wars. This pessimism he regards as historically anomalous. An example of his optimism is his rejection of political realism in Chap. 23, "The Unreality of 'Realism'," pp. 245-253; and chap. 24, "The Power of the Powerless," pp. 254-265. At p. 254: "Realism rests on two extremely shaky foundations: an impermissible reductionism concerning the motives and behavior of human societies, and failure to address the question of History."

29. See Fukuyama, especially Chap. 4, "The Worldwide Liberal Revolution," pp. 39-51, in which he documents the rise of liberal democracies worldwide across time; and Chap. 5, "An Idea for a Universal History," pp. 55-70, in which he argues for the philosophical possibility of "a meaningful pattern in the overall development of human societies generally." Fukuyama tracks a general decline of totalitarian regimes and ideologically-driven nation states.
Fukuyama formally distinguishes liberalism from democracy. "Political liberalism can be defined simply as a rule of law that recognizes certain individual rights and freedoms from government control," p. 42. Fukuyama focuses on civil, religious, and political rights. "Democracy, on the other hand, is the right held universally by all citizens to have a share of political power, that is, the right of all citizens to vote and participate in politics," p. 43. Fukuyama notes that although liberalism and democracy do not always go together, they usually do, and his view of the end of history finds them united.

30. When Fukuyama speaks of the end of history, he is speaking of the idea of "a coherent and directional History of mankind that will eventually lead the greater part of humanity to liberal democracy," p. xii. Fukuyama borrows heavily from Hegel, who viewed history as a rational process that "would come to an end with an achievement of free societies in the real world. This would, in other words, be *an end of history*. This did not mean that there would be an end to events arising out of births, deaths, and social interactions of humankind, or that there would be a cap on factual knowledge about the world. Hegel, however, had defined history as the progress of man to higher levels of rationality and freedom, and this process had a logical terminal point in the achievement of absolute self-consciousness," p. 64, emphasis in original.

31. *Ibid.*, p. xiv. See especially Chaps. 6-8, pp. 71-108.

32. Fukuyama anchors man's struggle for recognition in Plato's *thymos*, or spiritedness, a concept he sees embedded in many philosophical systems. For example, Hegel's "first man" desires "to be recognized as a *man*," which involves first and foremost his "ability to risk his own life," Fukuyama, p. 146. Closely connected to this desire to be esteemed and valued by others is the self-reflection of being worthy of such esteem, i.e., of being better than another. This desire to be regarded as superior to others Fukuyama terms *megalothymia*, calling its opposite, the desire to be regarded as the equal of others, *isothymia*. For a discussion of how *thymos* and *megalothymia* have led to war, and societies composed of slave and victor classes, see pp. 146-152, 181-198.

33. Fukuyama lauds Christianity as that religion which "first introduced the concept of the equality of all men in the sight of God, and thereby conceived of a shared destiny for all the peoples of the world," p. 56. He also criticizes Christianity because it relegated that vision of equality and freedom to the spiritual realm, judging the religion as "untrue in certain crucial respects," p. 197.

34. Fukuyama relates Hegel's critique of Christianity without dissent. "The last great slave ideology, Christianity, articulated for the slave a vision of what human freedom should be. Even though it did not provide him with a practical way out of his slavery, it permitted him to see more clearly his objective; the free and autonomous individual who is recognized for this freedom and autonomy, recognized universally and reciprocally by all men," Fukuyama, p. 198. Hegel believed that Christians were guilty of perpetuating a form of self-alienation by creating the concept of God, and then subordinating their "free wills" to that

God and to their temporal conditions through the retention of slave identities; see Fukuyama, pp. 195-197.

This assessment of Christianity turns on the power of the "free will" to choose and act. Historic Christian confessions have embraced the concept of a will which is empowered to choose and act freely, but only after Christ has come and first made it free.

35. See Fukuyama's discussion at pp. 195-199; quote at p. 195. It should be noted that for Fukuyama, it is only that absolutist quality of religion that, like nationalism, makes itself an obstacle to liberalism: "The second cultural obstacle to democracy has to do with religion. Like nationalism, there is no inherent conflict between religion and liberal democracy, except at the point where religion ceases to be tolerant and egalitarian," p. 216.

36. Fukuyama, pp. 300-312; quote at p. 300, emphasis in original. Here Fukuyama follows Nietzsche. If all men are absolutely free and equal, and all recognition is universal, what is the quality of such recognition? If the last man has plenteous security and luxury, if the last man has no values compelling enough to die for, and if striving and excellence require discontent, what will the end state of humanity be? On p. 336, Fukuyama concludes:

Looking around contemporary America, it does not strike me that we face the problem of an excess of *megalothymia*. Those earnest young people trooping off to law and business school, who anxiously fill out their résumés in hopes of maintaining the lifestyles to which they believe themselves entitled, seem to be much more in danger of becoming the last men, rather than reviving the passions of the first man.

37. That the loss of religion would coincide with the loss of true humanity suggests that Fukuyama's anthropology, based on economic and recognition privation, or positively on the need for economy and recognition, is inadequate. I believe Fukuyama's anthropology fails to take into account the fullness of the first man's privation. Beyond economy and recognition, man strives for love, hope, joy, reconciliation, righteousness, peace, and unending life—arguably the deliverables of religion. Unless the fullness of man participates in history, which itself is part of the history of effects, the fusion of history cannot achieve its final and rational end. This line of thinking suggests that unless the divine substantively enters into the human race to supply what is ontologically lacking, the history of effects cannot achieve a finally satisfying end, and there can be no end of history in Fukuyama's sense. Within Christian dogma, this entrance of the divine into human flesh is the Incarnation of the Son of God. For a superb analysis of the principle of the history of effects and the fusion of history at an end, see "The Elevation of the Historicity of Understanding to the Status of a Hermeneutical Principle," in Hans-Georg Gadamer's *Truth and Method*, 2d Rev. Ed., trans. revised by Joel Weinsheimer and Donald G. Marshall, New York: Continuum, 1988, pp. 265-307.

38. We would then "return to being first men engaged in bloody and pointless prestige battles, only this time with modern weapons." Fukuyama, p. 328.

39. *Ibid.*, pp. 322-327.

40. *Ibid.*, pp. 326-327.

41. Fukuyama uses the image of a wagon train to show the different evolutionary stages of societies and governments on the way to democratic liberalism and the end of history. "The apparent differences in the situations of the wagons will not be seen as reflecting permanent and necessary differences between the people riding in the wagons, but simply a product of their different positions along the road." That said, on the last page of *The End of History and the Last Man*, he stops short of guaranteeing a final universal destination of democratic liberalism, noting that, for now, "the direction of the wagons' wanderings must remain provisionally inconclusive," p. 339.

42. This is the point of Fukuyama, Chap. 26, "Toward a Pacific Union," pp. 276-284, particularly pp. 276-277:

For the foreseeable future, the world will be divided between a post-historical part, and a part that is still stuck in history. Within the post-historical world, the chief axis of interaction between states would be economic, and the old rules of power politics would have decreasing relevance.

. . . The historical world would still be riven with a variety of religious, national, and ideological conflicts depending on the stage of development of the particular countries concerned, in which the old rules of power politics continue to apply. Countries like Iraq and Libya will continue to invade their neighbors and fight bloody battles.

43. Fukuyama, p. 211.

44. *Ibid.,* p. 46.

45. *Ibid.,* p. 45.

46. *Ibid.,* p. 45. Fukuyama believes, however, that "the Islamic world would seem more vulnerable to liberal ideas in the long run than the reverse," p. 46.

47. Samuel P. Huntington, born in 1927, was a brilliant and conservative political scientist. He graduated from Yale at 18 and received his Ph.D. from Harvard at 23, at which time he began teaching in Harvard's Department of Government. His areas of study included national security; civil-military relations; and the role of culture in national identity, political governance, and international civilizations. He died on Christmas Eve of 2008. For a full biographical and professional background, see Robert Kaplan, "Looking the World in the Eye" *The Atlantic*, December 2001, available from *www.theatlantic.com/magazine/archive/2001/12/looking-the-world-in-the-eye/2354/.*

48. Huntington, p. 21. The three blocs were: states aligned with America, states aligned with the Soviet Union, and the remaining unaligned states.

49. *Ibid.,* p. 20; my emphasis.

50. *Ibid.,* p. 21.

51. *Ibid.,* Map 1.3, pp. 26-27, and discussion at pp. 45-48. The certain seven are: Western, Latin American, Islamic, Sinic (Chinese), Hindu, Orthodox, and Japanese. The possible eighth is African. Buddhism is excluded because "while Buddhism remains an important component of [certain] cultures, these societies do not constitute and would not identify themselves as part of a Buddhist civilization," p. 47.

52. *Ibid.,* p. 321.

53. For Huntington, fault line wars are violent communal conflicts fought between states or groups from different civilizations. Warring sides in fault line wars almost always come from different religions. For characteristics of fault line wars and communal wars, see pp. 252-254.

54. Huntington, p. 42.

55. *Ibid.,* p. 47. Although certain postmodern commentators may be offended by the claim that civilizations rest on religious foundations, consciences may be soothed by understanding the claim in its historical significance. One must ask which great civilizations were not founded on a profoundly religious understanding of identity, belief, and practice. It is another matter to bring such historical significance forward, to discuss whether a civilization's current identities, beliefs, and practices reflect those same foundations. It is yet another matter to ask whether, or to what extent, cohesive civilizations still exist today.

56. On references in this paragraph, see Huntington, p. 183. On the micro-macro distinction, see pp. 207-209. Huntington notes that "while at the macro or global level of world politics the primary clash of civilizations is between the West and the rest, at the micro or local level it is between Islam and the others," p. 255.

On the capitalization of "west" and "western," there is no single, authoritative literary convention. I follow the convention which capitalizes the proper nouns "West" and "Westerner," but not adjectival forms, when used to denote the generalized civilization and set of values associated with the United States and Europe. Huntington follows a different convention which additionally capitalizes the adjective "Western," reflected in quotations at notes 56 and 60.

57. Religion is clearly in view in the projected micro and macro level wars. Regarding Huntington's three contributing causes for projected dangerous wars, Islamic intolerance is overtly religious, western arrogance is derivatively religious, and Sinic assertiveness is least religious, and perhaps even nonreligious.

On Western arrogance and religious elements, see Chap. 7, "Core States, Concentric Circles, and Civilizational Order," pp. 155-179. Huntington builds the historic case that the civilizational roots of the West, to include those of the USA, lie in the Holy Roman Empire and western Christianity. He also charges that the West now arrogantly believes that its culture is universal, i.e., that the world should adapt its "superior" culture; see p. 310. For Huntington, the derived religious significance of western arrogance is adequately established by the fact that Islamic militants point to the West as "Christian" and urge Muslims to fight against it. Huntington does not go so far as to say that the arrogance of the West springs from its western Christian civilizational roots.

For a discussion of China's assertiveness as a function of its "history, culture, traditions, economic dynamism, and self-image," see Huntington, pp. 229-238.

58. Huntington capitalizes "Resurgence" in "Islamic Resurgence" because "it refers to an extremely important historical event affecting one-fifth or more of humanity, that is at least as significant as the American Revolution, French Revolution, or Russian Revolution, whose 'r's' are usually capitalized," p. 109.

59. Huntington, pp. 109-121.

60. *Ibid.*, pp. 109-110.

61. *Ibid.*, p. 111. Huntington notes correctly that this Resurgence is similar to the Protestant Reformation's effect on historic Christianity. If one defines the Protestant Reformation as the general reform movement in which Martin Luther and John Calvin stood as pillars, then that reformation was without doubt an attempt to return Christianity to its original, more pure religious foundations. It is interesting to note that there are a number of modern commentators who suggest that Islam, and radical Muslims today, are in need of a "reformation," using the term to signal a need for moderation and a less demanding form of piety. Use of this term in this sense demonstrates a failure to apprehend both the historical moorings and the effects of the Protestant Reformation. In the historic, theological sense, the goals of many radical Muslims today are reformational. For example, the view of the Taliban and al Qaeda is that they are calling Muslims to return to their historic religious beliefs and practices.

62. *Ibid.*, p. 121.

The Resurgence will leave a network of Islamist social, cultural, economic, and political organizations within societies and transcending societies. The Resurgence will also have shown that "Islam is the solution" to the problems of morality, identity, meaning, and faith, but not to the problems of social injustice, political repression, economic backwardness, and military weakness.

63. Huntington, pp. 174-179.

64. *Ibid.*, p. 174.

65. *Ibid.*, pp. 209-218.

66. *Ibid.*, p. 210. Huntington notes that "Islam is the only civilization which has put the survival of the West in doubt, and it has done that at least twice."

67. See Huntington's discussion of the Islam's bloody borders and related causes of war, pp. 254-265, especially pp. 262-265.

68. Huntington, p. 211.

69. Huntington's policy recommendations include recognizing civilizational differences, retooling current policies in that light, and abandoning all myths of universal culture, especially the myth that western culture is universal. For Huntington, part of recognizing civilizational differences means that the United States must, on the one hand, embrace its own identity as a western, and not a multicultural, civilization, and on the other hand, accept a multicultural world composed of multiple civilizations. Regarding the non-universal nature of the West, Huntington stands opposite to Fukuyama. See Huntington, pp. 308-321.

70. This restates my earlier contention that religion—not as a standard of belief, but as a power which drives human behavior—must have a seat at the table of national security policy, if that policy is to embrace the fullness of the human condition, and prove effective in the long run.

71. Robert Kaplan is an American journalist who has written extensively for *The Atlantic*. A well-traveled author and foreign correspondent, his trips to dangerous locations—including Iraq in 1984, Afghanistan in 1990, the Middle East, North Africa, Eastern Europe, and Central Asia—have helped him document a position that emphasizes cultural and environmental factors as decisive for post-Cold War national security. For further information and a list of his books, see his biography at *The Atlantic Online*, available from *www.theatlantic.com/past/unbound/kaplan/kapbio. htm,*.

72. Kaplan, p. 19; emphasis in original. On pp. 19-20, Kaplan continues,

The political and strategic impact of surging populations, spreading disease, deforestation and soil erosion, water depletion, air pollution, and, possibly, rising sea levels in critical, overcrowded regions like the Nile Delta and Bangladesh—developments that will prompt mass migrations and, in turn, incite group conflicts—will be the core foreign-policy challenge from which most others will ultimately emanate, arousing the public and uniting assorted interests left over from the Cold War.

For an opposing view on the threat of the environment, see Mark Steyn, *America Alone: The End of the World as We Know It*, Washington, DC: Regnery Publishing, 2006. Steyn argues that the insistence that the environment is the biggest national security issue for the future distracts the United States from the more concrete, deadlier threats that are accompanying changing Muslim demographics, especially in western Europe.

73. *Ibid.*, p. 24.

74. *Ibid.*, p. 22:

While a minority of the human population will be, as Francis Fukuyama would put it, sufficiently sheltered so as to enter a "post-historical" realm, living in cities and suburbs in which the environment has been mastered and ethnic animosities have been quelled by bourgeois prosperity, an increasingly large number of people will be stuck in history, living in shantytowns where attempts to rise above poverty, cultural dysfunction, and ethnic strife will be doomed by a lack of water to drink, soil to till, and space to survive in.

75. Based on personal experiences from his frequent travels, Kaplan illustrates friction between Muslims, and between Muslims and the West, anchoring the friction in cultural differences. In this sense, he usually subordinates religious animosities to cultural ones, but without denying the foundational religious clash. For example, on p. 29:

> Two months of recent travel throughout Turkey revealed to me that although the Turks are developing a deep distrust, bordering on hatred, of fellow-Muslim Iran, they are also, especially in the shantytowns that are coming to dominate Turkish public opinion, revising their group identity, increasingly seeing themselves as Muslims being deserted by a West that does little to help besieged Muslims in Bosnia and that attacks Turkish Muslims in the streets of Germany.

> In other words, the Balkans, a powder keg for nation-state war at the beginning of the twentieth century, could be a powder keg for cultural war at the turn of the twenty-first century: between Orthodox Christianity, represented by the Serbs and a classic Byzantine configuration of Greeks, Russians, and Romanians, and the House of Islam. Yet in the Caucasus that House of Islam is falling into a clash between Turkic and Iranian civilizations.

76. See Kaplan's discussion of Huntington's "Clash of Civilizations," pp. 26-30.

77. Kaplan, p. 35.

78. *Ibid.*, p. 35, quoting the 1951 work of Carleton Stevens Coon.

79. *Ibid.*, p. 35; emphasis in original. Kaplan does not discuss the doctrine of *jihad*. Rather, in the context of environmental crises and failing states, he sees Islam as providing the political framework—to include forms of extremism—that will gain traction among Muslims. "Much of the Arab world . . . will undergo alteration, as Islam spreads across artificial frontiers, fueled by mass migrations into the cities and a soaring birth rate. . . . As state control mechanisms wither in the face of environmental and demographic stress, 'hard' Islamic city-states or shantytown-states are likely to emerge." pp. 41-42.

His view of the result across Islamic lands—part of the coming anarchy—leads Kaplan to conclude that maps of the world of nation states will be obsolete. In a nice parody of Fukuyama, Kaplan discusses "The Last Map," pp. 50-56.

80. Kaplan, p. 32. See pp. 30-37 for Kaplan's discussion of the successes of Turkey's secular government, built on a powerful Turkish Muslim culture. At p. 36: "Turkey has been living through the Muslim equivalent of the Protestant Reformation." Here Kaplan presents a positive view of the secular Turkish government and what he characterizes as its moderating, modernizing, and stabilizing effects. For additional information on Turkey's current struggles, see note 154 below. From an historical and theological perspective, Kaplan is misguided in using the Protestant Reformation as a framework for such effects; see note 61 above.

81. See Chap. 2, "Was Democracy Just a Moment?" in Kaplan, pp. 59-98. For Kaplan, democracies are inherently value-neutral and do not necessarily make societies more civil, at least not in the short run; see pp. 61-63. He suggests that in certain circumstances it may make sense to sacrifice justice for the sake of order. This could mean supporting a tyrannical regime, where grave injustices are perpetuated in the name of religion. Kaplan follows Kissinger in arguing that, in the final analysis, "disorder is worse than injustice," p. 134. As a policy example, consider Kaplan's "Third World aid policy" based on proportionalism, where the evil endured is outweighed by the good accomplished; see pp. 121-122.

82. Kaplan, p. 93. Kaplan applies this principle in multiple contexts—ancient, postmodern, national, and international—concluding that "the category of politics we live with may depend more on power relationships and the demeanor of our society than on whether we hold elections," p. 96.

83. By "faith dimension" I mean religion as a comprehensive set of beliefs about God, which interprets the past, integrates human longings across time, and brings the world to fulfillment. This faith dimension includes ontology and epistemology. Religion as an ontological system generally begins with a conceptual essence of God and proceeds outward to include humanity and the world. Since the Enlightenment, religion as an epistemological method generally begins with the experiences of humanity and works its way toward God. In my analysis of Islam, I focus on religion as an ontological system. This approach aligns with the inner structure of the religion of Islam.

84. I am indebted to Dr. Adam Francisco for his help in navigating the vast sea of available works on Islam. His bibliographical expertise proved invaluable in Section II of this manuscript. Dr. Francisco studied Arabic and Islamic Theology at the Centre for Islamic Studies, University of Oxford, receiving his D.Phil. for his work in the history of Christian-Muslim relations.

I have relied on a number of resources. For a general overview of Islam and the significance of the *Qur'an* and the *Sunnah*, see John L. Esposito, *Islam: The Straight Path*, Rev. 3d Ed., updated with new epilogue, New York: Oxford University Press, 2005; Daniel Madigan, "Themes and Topics," in *Cambridge Companion to the Qur'an*, Cambridge, UK: Cambridge University Press, 2006, pp. 79-96; Sayyid Abul A'la Maududi, *Toward Understanding Islam*, Rev. Ed., Khurshid Ahmed, trans. and ed., no publication data, 1960; Fazlur Rahman, *Major Themes of the Qur'an*, Minneapolis, MN: Bibliotheca Islamica, 1980; Tariq Ramadan, *Western Muslims and the Future of Islam*, New York: Oxford University Press, 2004; Efraim Karsh, *Islamic Imperialism: A History*, Updated Ed., New Haven: Yale University Press, 2007.

On *usul al-fiqh* (principles of Islamic jurisprudence), *Shari'ah* (divine law), and *fatwas* (legal rulings), see Mohammad Hashim Kamali, *Principles of Islamic Jurisprudence*, 3d Rev. and enlarged Ed., Cambridge, UK: The Islamic Texts Society, 2003.

On *siyar* (the Islamic law of nations), see Khadduri, first cited in note 4 above. Khadduri provides superb analysis of Shaybani, "the most important jurist to write on the *siyar*," p. 22. For a transmission of the classical traditionalist *siyar*, see Muhammad Hamidullah, *The Muslim Conduct of State*, Rev. and enlarged Wd., Lahore, Pakistan: Sh. Muhammad Ashraf, 1968. For a modern interpretive view of *siyar*, compare Labeeb Ahmed Bsoul, *International Treaties (Mu'ahadat) in Islam: Theory and Practice in the Light of Islamic International Law (Siyar) According to Orthodox Schools*, Lanham, MD: University Press of America, 2008.

On *jihad* (struggle or war), see all the above resources for the foundations of *jihad* in the *Qur'an*, *Sunnah*, *Shari'ah*, and constructs within *usul al-fiqh* and *siyar*. For the most comprehensive modern history and primary source compilation regarding *jihad*, see Bostom, first cited in note 4 above. In addition, see Shmuel Bar, *Warrant for Terror: Fatwas of Radical Islam and the Duty of Jihad*, Lanham, MD: Rowman & Littlefield, Inc., 2006; David Cook, *Understanding Jihad*, Berkeley, CA: University of California Press, 2005.

On English spelling, there are many ways of transliterating from the Arabic. I italicize and generally follow the formally correct transliterations of Kamali. This means that direct quotes from other authors may introduce different spellings, based on their personal preferences. Certain authors do not use italics for Arabic words, a standard convention for foreign language words. In such cases, for the sake of consistency I italicize the Arabic words, even in direct quotes, noting in the end note, "my italics." (This is different from end note references to "my emphasis," which marks my addition of italicized text in a quote *as my emphasis*, rather than as a foreign language.)

85. I offer the comparison with Christianity as a frame of reference, because most readers of this manuscript will certainly be from the western or Christian tradition.

86. Out of respect, Islam capitalizes "Prophet" when referring to Muhammad. Quote from Esposito, p. 17.

87. See Esposito, pp. 17-20, on the radical nature of Islam's monotheism. God is radically transcendent and exists as Unity in himself, apart from his creation. The *Qur'an* serves to bring the law—*Shari'ah*—which, in turn, effects the rule of God. By obedience to this law, the Muslim submits to God as God. This law defines the Muslim and his life. A human becomes a Muslim through submission to the law of this radically transcendent God. This submission initially occurs by confessing the *shahada* (testimony), "There is no god but God and Muhammad is the Prophet of God." The *shahada* is the first so-called pillar of Islam,

signifying agreement with two propositions: Allah alone is to be worshiped, and Muhammad is the final and perfect Messenger of that God. The other pillars are *salat* (prayer), *zakat* (alms), *sawm* (fasting), and *hajj* (pilgrimage). On the five pillars and their centrality for Islamic life and practice, see Esposito, pp. 68-114.

88. The variety of forms and lack of chronology lead to interpretive difficulties, which are discussed below.

89. This distinction is important, as the Meccan passages enjoin peaceful behavior, while the Medinan verses generally enjoin war.

90. The *Sunnah* is regarded as revelation but it is qualitatively different than *Qur'anic* revelation. The *Qur'an* is viewed as God's eternal and unerring word. The utterances and deeds of Muhammad are revelatory in the sense that they are inspired, but not necessarily inerrant.

91. Out of respect, Islam capitalizes "Companions," based on their closeness to the Prophet.

92. The *sirah*, the biographical accounts of Muhammad's life, draw heavily upon the *hadith*. The earliest *sirah* was written by Ibn Ishaq's Sirat al-Rasul Allah, but this work is no longer extant. A redaction of it does exist (from Ibn Hisham, 9th century) available in an English translation: *The Life of Muhammad: A Translation of Ibn Ishaq's Sirat Rasul Allah*, trans. and annot. by Alfred Guillame, London, UK: Oxford University Press, 1955.

93. *Shari'ah* was never a codified, completed body of law. Instead, it includes the *Qur'an* and *Sunnah*, together with the discussions, commentaries, and *fatwas* of authorized Islamic legal experts, as authoritative practice for the *ummah*. See Kamali, pp. 16-186.

94. For an overview of the relation of *usul al-fiqh* to *Shari'ah*, and *usul al-fiqh*'s location within the broader Islamic sciences, see Ramadan, pp. 55-61. Note especially the helpful chart at p. 57.

95. Within radical Islam, *fatwas* are frequently used to justify *jihad* and acts of terror. See Bar's volume which superbly documents this use of *fatwas* in the modern period.

96. The *Sunnah* attest to these revelations, through the utterances and deeds of Muhammad.

97. For examples of the liberal position, see the discussion of John L. Esposito; and of the postmodern position, see Tariq Ramadan.

98. From Ibn Warraq's foreward in Bostom, p. 23.

99. For an introduction to the meanings and usages of the word *jihad*, see Rudolph Peters, "Jihad: An Introduction," in Bostom, pp. 320-325. Although *jihad* in its most basic sense means "to strive, to exert oneself, to struggle," Peters notes that most occurrences in the *Qur'an* and among the Islamic jurists carry the sense of "armed struggle against the unbelievers," p. 320.

100. Khadduri, p. 5. Khadduri communicates the perspective of a devout Muslim. In explaining Islamic military aggression, he understands the motivation as religious zeal for the conversion of those who would be conquered. Khadduri subordinates any expansionistic desire to this religious motivation.
Certain liberal Islamic apologists note that Christianity has no less a universal vision of its faith and similarly seeks the conversion of the world. This is true, as far as it goes. But such a comparison fails to account for historical distinctions, i.e., for Islam's norm of submission through warfare and Christianity's norm of conversion through proclamation. The former worked through external domination, the latter through internal affection. This is not to deny that historic Islam desired, sought, and achieved conversion through proclamation, but to recognize that such was a penultimate means, with external *jihad* providing the final means, at least for the initial Islamic centuries.

101. See Khadduri, pp. 10-14, for the classical position. Like Khadduri, Bsoul follows Shaybani as the definitive commentator on *siyar* in the classical tradition. See Bsoul, pp. 14-26, for his discussion of *dar al-Islam* and *dar al-harb*, covering both classical and reformed perspectives, with more of an evolutionary approach to law. Bar, pp. 18-24, also covers the classical and reformed perspectives, with greater emphasis on the effects for the *ummah*. For the additions of *dar al-ahd* (the territory of treaty), *dar al-amn* (territory of safety), and *dar al-dawa* (territory of invitation), see Ramadan, pp. 66-75.

102. Khadduri, p. 12.

103. Quote from Khadduri, p. 13. On the conditions for temporarily halting hostilities, see Khadduri, pp. 5-14, and Bsoul, p. ix.

104. Khadduri, p. 15; my italics.

105. Hamidullah, paragraph 312, p. 163. This is not to claim that the benefits do not accrue to the individual for participation in *jihad*. Those who undertake *jihad* receive both the spoils of war, and the rewards of Paradise. Indeed there is no more certain way in classical Islam to inherit Paradise than to participate in *jihad*. See Khadduri, note 28, at p.p 15, 72; and Chap. 3 in Shabaybani's *Siyar*; Khadduri, pp. 106-129.

106. *Qur'an* 9:111, *Sahih International*, available from *quran.com/9/111*. At the same location, see the *Tafsir al-Jalalayn* commentary on the first part of the verse:

> Indeed God has purchased from the believers their lives and their possessions, that they expend it in obedience of Him—for example by striving in His way—so that theirs will be [the reward of] Paradise: they shall fight in the way of God and they shall kill and be killed, this sentence is independent and constitutes an explication of the [above-mentioned] "purchase"; a variant reading has the passive verb come first [sc. *fa-yuqtalūna wa-yaqtulūn*, "they shall be killed and shall kill"], meaning that some of them are killed while those who remain, fight on.

107. *Qur'an* 9:5, *Sahih International*, available from *quran.com/9/5*. At the same location, see *Tafsir al-Jalalayn* commentary on the first part of the verse:

> Then, when the sacred months have passed—that is, [at] the end of the period of deferment—slay the idolaters wherever you find them, be it during a lawful [period] or a sacred [one], and take them, captive, and confine them, to castles and forts, until they have no choice except [being put to] death or [acceptance of] Islam.

108. *Qur'an* 9:29, *Sahih International*, available from *quran.com/9/2,*; my italics. At the same location, see *Tafsir al-Jalalayn* commentary on the first part of the verse:

> Fight those who do not believe in God, nor in the Last Day, for, otherwise, they would have believed in the Prophet(s), and who do not forbid what God and His Messenger have forbidden, such as wine, nor do they practise the religion of truth, the firm one, the one that abrogated other religions, namely, the religion of Islam—from among of those who, *min*, "from," explains [the previous] *alladhīna* "those who," have been given the Scripture, namely, the Jews and the Christians, until they pay the jizya tribute, the annual tax imposed them, readily, *an yadin* is a circumstantial qualifier, meaning, "compliantly," or "by their own hands," not delegating it [to others to pay], being subdued, [being made] submissive and compliant to the authority of Islam.

It is true that within conquered lands under *Shari'ah*, Jews and Christians were allowed to live as second class citizens, provided they paid the annual tax. Their status, called *dhimmitude*, was frequently characterized by repression. For a comprehensive survey of *dhimmitude* with hundreds of historical examples, see Andrew G. Bostom, "*Jihad* Conquests and the Imposition of Dhimmitude—A Survey," in Bostom, pp. 24-124.

109. *Qur'an* 4:95, *Sahih International*, available from *quran.com/4/95*, my italics. The phrase, "with their wealth and their lives," implies that the true *jihad* is that struggle whereby one gives his wealth to support Islamic war and follows up this support by fighting as a combatant. At the same location, see the *Tafsir al-Jalalayn* commentary on the verse:

> The believers who sit at home, away from the struggle, other than those who have an injury, such as a chronic illness or blindness or the like, read in the nominative, *ghayru ūlī l-darar*, "other than those who have an injury," as an adjectival clause; or in the accusative, *ghayra ūlī l-darar* (as an exceptive clause) are not the equals of those who struggle in the way of God with their possessions and their lives. God has preferred those who struggle with their possessions and their lives over the ones who sit at home, on account of some injury, by a degree, by [a degree of] merit, since both have the same intention, but the extra degree is given to those who have carried out the struggle; yet to each, of the two groups, God has promised the goodly reward, Paradise, and God has preferred those who struggle over the ones who sit at home, without any injury, with a great reward, *ajran 'azīman*, is substituted by [the following, *darajātin minhu*].

110. *Qur'an* 8:39, *Sahih International*, available from *quran.com/8/39*, my italics. At the same location, see *Tafsir al-Jalalayn* commentary on the verse: "And fight them until sedition, idolatry, is, exists, no more and religion is all for God, alone, none other being worshipped; then if they desist, from unbelief, surely God sees what they do, and will requite them for it."

111. See M. K. Kister, "The Massacre of the Banu Qurayza: A Re-examination of a Tradition," *Jerusalem Studies in Arabic and Islam*, Vol. 8, 1986, pp. 61-96. For a summary of Kister, see Bostom, pp. 17-19.

112. Muhammad ibn Umar al-Waqidi, *Kitab al-Maghazi*, London, UK: Oxford University Press, Vol. 3, 1966, p. 1113.

113. *Qur'an* 22:78, *Sahih International*, available from *quran.com/22/78*, my italics. At the same location, see the *Tafsir al-Jalalayn* commentary on the verse:

> And struggle in the way of God, in order to establish His religion, a struggle worthy of Him, by expending all effort therein, *haqqa* is in the accusative because it is a verbal noun. He has elected you, He has chosen you for His religion, and has not laid upon you in your religion any hardship, that is, [any] constraint, for He has facilitated [adherence to] it during times of difficulty, such as [His permitting you] to shorten prayers, to seek ritual purification from earth, to eat of carrion, and to break the fast during illness or travel—the creed of your father, *millata* is in the accusative because the genitive preposition *kāf* [sc. *ka-millati*, "like the creed of"] has been omitted. Abraham, *Ibrāhīma*, an explicative supplement. He, that is, God, named you Muslims before, that is, before [the revelation of] this Book, and in this, that is, [in] the *Qur'ān*, so that the Messenger might be a witness against you, on the Day of Resurrection, that he delivered the Message to you, and that you might be witnesses against mankind, that their messengers delivered the Message to them. So maintain prayer, observe it regularly, and pay the alms, and hold fast to God, trust in Him. He is your Patron, your Helper and the Guardian of your affairs. An excellent Patron, is He, and an excellent Helper, for you.

114. *Qur'an* 9:81, *Sahih International*, available from *quran.com/9/81*. At the same location, see the *Tafsir al-Jalalayn* commentary on the verse:

> Those who were left behind, from [the journey to] Tabūk, rejoiced at remaining behind the Messenger of God, and were averse to striving with their wealth and their lives in the way of God. And they said, that is, they said to one another, "Do not go forth, do not set off to [join] the fight, in the heat!" Say "The fire of Hell is hotter, than Tabūk, and more worthy for them to guard against, by not staying behind, did they but understand," this, they would not have stayed behind.

115. *Qur'an* 2:256, *Sahih International*, available from *quran.com/2/256*, my italics. Note that although this verse does not use the word *jihad*, or a derivative, the verse is frequently invoked to argue that true *jihad* is non-violent. At the same location, see the *Tafsir al-Jalalayn* commentary on the verse:

> There is no compulsion in, entering into, religion. Rectitude has become clear from error, that is to say, through clear proofs it has become manifest that faith is rectitude and disbelief is error: this was revealed concerning the *Ansār* [of Medina] who tried to compel their sons to enter into Islam; so whoever disbelieves in the false deity, namely, Satan or idols, *tāghūt*, "false deity," is used in a singular and plural sense, and believes in God, has laid hold of the most firm handle, the tight knot, unbreaking, that cannot be severed; God is Hearing, of what is said, Knowing, of what is done.

116. I have based much of my discussion of the greater and lesser *jihad* on Cook, pp. 32-48. Quote at p. 35; my italics. It appears that the "greater *jihad*," as an inner and spiritual struggle, is documented only after the initial military expansion of Islam stalled.

117. Such a possible synthesis assumes the enduring validity of *jihad* as warfare. Khadduri explains this as follows: "The believers may fulfill the *jihad* duty by heart in their efforts to combat the devil and to escape his persuasion to evil; by their tongue and hands in their attempt to support the right and correct the wrong; and by the sword in taking part in actual fighting and by sacrificing their 'wealth and lives,'" pp. 15-16, note 29, my italics.

118. On *naskh*, see Kamali, pp. 202-227. "Abrogation applies almost exclusively to the *Qur'an* and the *Sunnah*," p. 203. Most Islamic legal scholars believe that *naskh* exists and applies within the *Qur'an*. Six juridical conditions must be satisfied before *naskh* can be applied. For a discussion of these six conditions, see Kamali, p. 207. The first stipulation is that the "text itself has not precluded the possibility of abrogation." Kamali notes that *jihad* can never be abrogated "because the *hadith* . . . proclaims that '*jihad* shall remain valid till the day of resurrection'."

119. Kamali, pp. 24-25, anchors the permissibility of *jihad* in the later Medinan revelations. Also see Raymond Ibrahim, "How Taqiyya Alters Islam's Rules of War," *The Middle East Quarterly*, Vol. 17, No. 1, Winter 2010, available from *www.meforum.org/2538/taqiyya-islam-rules-of-war*. Ibrahim notes,

> The [Islamic legal scholars] were initially baffled as to which verses to codify into the *Shari'a* worldview—the one that states there is no coercion in religion (2:256), or the ones that command believers to fight all non-Muslims till they either convert, or at least submit, to Islam (8:39, 9:5, 9:29). To get out of this quandary, the commentators developed the doctrine of abrogation, which essentially maintains that verses revealed later in Muhammad's career take precedence over earlier ones whenever there is a discrepancy. In order to document which verses abrogated which, a religious science devoted to the chronology of the Qur'an's verses evolved (known as *an-Nasikh wa'l Mansukh*, the abrogater and the abrogated).

Another important dialog within Islam, which parallels the dynamics of the applicability of *naskh*, is the discussion of whether legitimate *jihad* is defensive or offensive in nature. Interpreters emphasizing the defensive posture cite earlier Qur'anic passages, while those justifying offensive actions cite the later revelations. A credible argument for defensive *jihad* may be made theologically, but not historically. Islamic clerics sometimes see a theological principle at work, where that portion of humanity which has not submitted to Allah is in truth attacking the universalizing work of the *ummah* and the will of Allah. In this theological sense, the Islamic invasion of foreign lands may be construed to be defensive in nature. That said, the historical perspective of Islamic warfare expanding to take the fight into Spain, France, and Italy cannot credibly be called defensive.

120. See Bar, pp. 2-3, for *naskh* as the questionable basis for terrorist *fatwas*.
Within the discussion of the priority of the *Qur'anic* Medinan texts over the early Meccan texts, and

of the militant over the peaceful *jihad*, it is important to call attention to an intensifying factor frequently present in such interpretations. This is the apocalyptic factor. See Cook, pp. 22-25, for a discussion of how Islamic military expansion may have been tied to popular views that the world was about to end. Cook extends this line of thought in his analysis of modern radical Islam; see pp. 157-161.

See also Timothy R. Furnish, *Holiest Wars: Islamic Mahdis, their Jihads, and Osama bin Laden*, Westport, CT: Praeger Publishing, 2005. He documents Islamic eschatology and the rise of *Mahdism*—the belief that a messiah, *al-Mahdi*, would reveal himself and usher in a worldwide Islamic state. Furnish tracks eight *Mahdi* movements within *Sunni* Islam. He also briefly discusses *Shi'i* Muslims who look for the Hidden Imam to reveal himself and usher in the final universalization of Islam. Many terrorists subscribe to such *Mahdist* views, and believe that their attacks, both against the West and against heterodox Muslims, will usher in the final Islamic fulfillment.

121. In no way do I intend the use of the term "problem" to be derogatory. When I speak of the "problem" of Islam, or of any religion for that matter, I mean that religion's essential framework for understanding God and integrating a problematic humanity within that framework. In short, the problem of a religion propels the structure of that religion to deliver the power of that religion.

An example which may prove helpful for western audiences would be the problem of Christianity. The "problem" of Christianity is arguably the problem of love. Christianity conceives of the essential nature of God as love, with all other conceptions such as justice subordinated within the Godhead. This love exists within the one God himself, in the relation of the Persons of Father, Son, and Spirit. For the Christian: Father, Son, Spirit is God, and there is no God but Father, Son, and Spirit. Love binds Father and Son together in the unity of the Spirit. The problematic nature of love is seen in fallen humanity's failure to love God and one's neighbor purely and fully. The solution to the problem occurs in the enfleshment of the Son, who suffers and overcomes humanity's failures and fallenness. This Son sends his Spirit through word and baptism to create faith and graft humanity into his own body. Connected with God's love through the Son, humanity begins to love God and neighbor aright. This example shows how the "problem" of Christianity propels the structure of Christianity to deliver the power of Christianity.

122. This truth applies to the individual, the *ummah*, and the world.

123. This does not deny the internal, spiritual struggle that *jihad* also implied, and continues to imply. Rather, it emphasizes the continuing potential for legitimate, violent *jihad*.

124. My six categories overlap somewhat with Esposito's four categories, from which I have drawn some of my materials. See Esposito, pp. 228-232. Esposito divides the Islam of today into four categories—secularist, conservative, neotraditionalist, and reformist. The apparent similarity with my nomenclature, however, may be deceiving. Esposito's overarching purpose is to articulate how groups or positions within Islam address the need for change within Islam. Based on this approach, Esposito does not discuss radical traditionalist Islam as a position within Islam; this position sees no need to modernize the assumptions of historic Islam. Instead, Esposito speaks of a "radical activist" segment, which category largely overlaps my category of radical traditionalist Islam. See Esposito, p. 166. Esposito also fails to distinguish the liberal and postmodern reformed positions, perhaps because both include a concept of change which addresses modern, political processes.

My approach differs from Esposito's. My overarching purpose here is not to address perceptions about Islam's need for change, but to articulate how groups or positions within Islam today address the central question of the Islamic faith—how Islam is to achieve its universalization. That Esposito addresses another question which is central neither to the *Qur'an* nor to Muhammad as we know him from the *Sunnah* and his biographies—i.e, how Islam is to change—is a reflection of Esposito and his assumptions from the liberal reformed position.

125. Regarding the naming of Islamic positions, I find certain terms currently in use to be less than helpful. For example, is an "extremist" one who is simply taking a good idea too far, i.e., to the extreme? If so, how far ought he to take his good idea? If "*jihadists*" are those Muslims who take *jihad* seriously, would not this term necessarily apply to all faithful Muslims, irrespective of variances in their particular under-

standings of *jihad*? What about "fundamentalists"? Are these people who subscribe to the fundamentals of their faith? If so, what religious adherent would want to subscribe to something other than that which was fundamental for that faith? "Islamists" and "Islamicists" are equally problematic terms, attempting to create a pejorative for a certain party within Islam, without identifying the distinctive nature of that party. Names matter and should articulate what is distinctive about the position being named.

126. On the distinctions between Wahhabists and Salifists, the often unexpected alliances between *Sunni* and *Shi'ah* groups, and the significant ideological differences within the broader radical Arab *Sunni* population, see Samuel Helfont, *The Sunni Divide: Understanding Politics and Terrorism in the Arab Middle East*, Philadelphia, PA: Foreign Policy Research Institute, 2009. Helfont's work is published under the Foreign Policy Research Institute's Center on Terrorism and Counterterrorism, available from *www.fpri.org/pubs/Helfont.SunniDivide.pdf*.

There are multiple ways to transliterate words affiliated with *Sunni* and *Shi'ah* Islam. I follow the usages of Furnish and Kamali, which seem to represent the Arabic most faithfully. For the collective name of the sects, when used either as a noun or adjective, I use *Sunni* and *Shi'ah*. For the name of an adherent, when used either as a noun or adjective, I use *Sunni* and *Shi'i*. For the plural form of adherents, I use *Sunnis* and *Shi'is*.

127. On radical Islam and contemporary *jihad* theory, see Cook, pp. 93-127. On Osama bin Laden and global radical Islam, see Cook, pp. 128-161; and Esposito, pp. 262-263.

128. Inter-Islamic warfare often breaks down into *Shi'ah* versus *Sunni*. This historic divide within Islam has erupted into war countless times. It is also true that Abd al-Wahhab considered "the overwhelming majority of Muslims as infidels," and that many Wahhabists today make similar judgments; see Helfont, p. 5. The scale of potential *Shi'ah-Sunni* sectarian violence was graphically manifested following the 2006 bombing of the *Al 'Askari* mosque in Samarra, Iraq.

129. See Helfont, pp. 25-52, for a review of various terrorist organizations throughout the Middle East. Helfont's study is chiefly structured against the backdrop of the *Sunni* division between the Muslim Brotherhood and Wahhabists, but does take into account *Shi'i* Iran and its drive for regional hegemony.

130. *Qur'an* 4:29, *Sahih International*, available from *quran.com/4/29*. "O you who have believed, do not consume one another's wealth unjustly but only [in lawful] business by mutual consent. And do not kill yourselves [or one another]. Indeed, Allah is to you ever Merciful."

131. See Cook, pp. 142-147. Cook views with skepticism the applicability of such *Qur'anic* passages quoted by Islamic terrorists. Cook notes that even if one grants the permissibility of martyrdom operations within Islam, there still remains the problem of legitimate authorization for undertaking terrorist attacks and, for that matter, any militant *jihad*. Radical Muslim movements "disregard the necessity of established authority," for the history of Islam shows that only "a legitimate authority such as a caliph or an *imam* could declare *jihad*"(p. 164). The radical Muslim, however, finds the needed authorization in *fatwas* produced to address precisely this dilemma.

132. See Khadduri, pp. 57-59, on adjustments to the Islamic concept of *jihad* in light of Islam's relative loss of power.

133. See Khadduri, pp. 20-21, 57-70, on adjustments to the Islamic concept of universalization, due to geopolitical realities.

134. Kamali, p. 501.

135. *Ibid.*, p. 504.

136. *Ibid.*, p. 513.

137. This list follows the analysis of Esposito, pp. 229-231.

138. For example, consider the Muslim Brotherhood. Helfont points out that the Brotherhood has taken a more political than theological approach in addressing Islamic conflict, and has recognized the principle of nonviolence. Nonetheless, its sanctioned practice includes suicide bombings and other terrorist tactics. "In several cases, such as in Iraq and Afghanistan, the Muslim Brotherhood's understanding of *jihad* represents a direct military threat to the U.S. and its allies," p. 53, my italics.

139. For another postmodern vision of Islam, see Abdulaziz Sachedina, *The Islamic Roots of Democratic Pluralism*, New York: Oxford University Press, 2001.

140. See Ramadan, pp. 3-7. "There is one Islam, and the fundamental principles that define it are those to which all Muslims adhere, even though there may be, clothed in Islamic principles, an important margin allowed for evolution, transformation, and adaptation to various social and cultural environments," p. 9.

141. *Ibid.*, p. 14.

142. Ramadan is representative of the postmodern Muslim position, for he rejects traditionalist understandings of *Shari'ah* as a defined set of rules and of *jihad* as an external struggle. Instead he views *Shari'ah* as "the path that leads to the spring," p. 31. On p. 113, he characterizes *jihad* as those

> . . . individual and collective efforts, *jihads*, to be made at various levels and in various areas. On the intimate level, it is working on one's self, mastering one's egoisms and one's own violence; on the social level, it is the struggle for greater justice and against various kinds of discrimination, unemployment, and racism; on the political level, it is the defense of civil responsibilities and rights and the promotion of pluralism, freedom of expression, and the democratic processes; on the economic level, it is action against speculation, monopolies, and neocolonialism; on the cultural level, it is the promotion of the arts and forms of expression that respect the dignity of conscience and human values.

143. Ramadan, p. 17. For Ramadan, because none of the constitutive elements of man is positive or negative in itself, no external battle to achieve unity makes sense. Instead, the responsible conscience will seek the original testimony of the traces of the Creator left within man. In this way Ramadan moves the basis for Islamic unity from outside man to within man. See Ramadan, pp. 14-19.

144. *Ibid.*, p. 151; emphasis in original.

145. *Ibid.*, pp. 148-152.

146. *Ibid.*, p. 214: "Islam stands as a civilization as a result of this singular ability to express its universal and fundamental principles across the spread of history and geography while integrating the diversity and taking on the customs, tastes, and styles that belong to the various cultural contexts." The nomenclature of "Islamic civilization" raises Huntington's thesis. To a degree, Ramadan resonates with this thesis. On p. 226, he notes that,

> . . . if the clash is not a reality, the ingredients that could lead to it are very present in current mentalities; on both sides, the lack of knowledge of the other (and of self), the acceptance of simplistic and absolute caricatures and final judgments, not to mention conflicting political and geostrategic interests, are objective features that could lead to the breakdown.

Interestingly, Ramadan concludes that the West will not likely meet Islam at the "geopolitical frontiers." Rather, to preclude a breakdown, it will be "within European and American societies" where successful listening and dialog must occur.

147. John L. Esposito is a Professor of Islamic Studies and the Founding Director of the Prince Alwaleed bin Talal Center for Muslim-Christian Understanding at the Walsh School of Foreign Service, Georgetown University. The Prince Alwaleed bin Talal Center for Muslim-Christian Understanding was founded in December 2005 through a $20 million dollar gift from Prince Alwaleed Bin Talal of Saudi Arabia. Previously the institute existed as the Center for Muslim-Christian Understanding.

148. The assumptions of theological liberalism inform Esposito's method of analyzing Islam.

149. Esposito, p. 12.

150. *Ibid.*, my emphasis.

151. *Ibid.*, pp. 13-14. Esposito further interprets *jihad* today as the broader "religious, intellectual, spiritual, and moral" struggle to bring Muslims into "a progressive, constructive, modern Islamic framework in response to the realities of Muslim societies," pp. 266-267.

152. *Ibid.*, p. 31.

153. Western political leaders have frequently hailed such a vision as a welcome basis for finding common cause with Islamic nation states. Interestingly, Esposito goes out of his way to note that Islam, Christianity, Judaism, and Hinduism have each been wrongfully accused of supporting terrorism; see p. 270. This is true as far as it goes, but Esposito fails to note certain critical historical distinctions among the religions. For example, unlike Jesus, Muhammad was a warrior who commanded his followers to wage war. That Esposito omits this demonstrates that his method is more committed to transhistorical principles than to historical data.

For an opposing view to Esposito, see Michael Scheuer, *Imperial Hubris: Why the West Is Losing the War on Terror*, with new epilogue, Dulles, VA: Potomac Books, 2005. Scheuer argues that traditionalist Muslims will not give up their ideology to embrace the liberal perspective that all ideologies are essentially equal.

154. For a critical snapshot of the challenges that continue to face Egypt, consider that 53 percent of Muslims in Egypt find terrorist actions to be justifiable in defense of Islam, under certain situations. See related discussion at Table 8. For a discussion of the political mobilization of Islam in Mubarak's Egypt, see Carrie Rosefsky Wickham, *Mobilizing Islam: Religion, Activism, and Political Change in Egypt*, New York: Columbia University Press, 2002.

Regarding Turkey and the rise of the Justice and Development Party (AKP) beginning in 2002, see Morton Abramowitz and Henri J. Barkley, "Turkey's Political Revolution: Ankara's Civil-Military Struggle Has Global Significance," *The Wall Street Journal*, March 22, 2010, available from *online.wsj.com/article/SB1000142 405274870420750457512931343466900.html?mod=WSJ_Opinion_LEFTTopBucket*. The article documents the threat of the evolution of Turkey from a secular democracy to a more religious and authoritarian state. For a similar discussion of current pressures to move Turkey toward Islamic nation state status, see Bassam Tibi, "Islamists Approach Europe: Turkey's Islamist Danger," *The Middle East Quarterly*, Vol. 16, No. 1, Winter 2009, available from *www.meforum.org/2047/islamists-approach-europe?gclid=CP684dLJw6ACFcN05Q odLjMhZw*. For another discussion of secular-state Turkey confronting a challenge to move toward a more Islamic government and still remain pluralistic, see M. Hakan Yavuz and John L. Esposito, eds., *Turkish Islam and the Secular State: The Gülen Movement*, Syracuse, NY: Syracuse University Press, 2003.

155. See Thomas F. Lynch III, *Sunni and Shi'a Terrorism: Differences that Matter*, Occasional Paper Series, West Point Combating Terrorism Center, December 29, 2008, available from *gsmcneal. com/wp-content/up-loads/2008/12/sunni-and-shia-terrorism-differences-that-matter.pdf*.

156. *Ibid.*, p. 64. On *Shi'i* "campaigns" versus *Sunni* "waves," see especially charts on pp. 23, 28. Lynch offers policy recommendations that address *Sunni* and *Shi'i* terrorism as discrete threats; see pp. 59-65.

Lynch offers a list of *Sunni* and *Shi'i* terror organizations, many of which he references in his study; see pp. 66-72.

157. Helfont, p. 1.

158. *Ibid.*, my italics. Helfont finds these Sunni divisions to be "generally indicative of the political order in the Middle East," p. 1.

159. See Helfont, pp. 4-8, for his discussion of Wahhabism.

160. Wahhabism identifies Saudi Arabia as its ideological home, and continues to have a strong presence there.

161. See Helfont, pp. 8-23, for his discussion of the Muslim Brotherhood.

162. For a comparison of the Muslim Brotherhood and Wahhabism, with special attention to differences in their concept of *jihad*, see Helfont, pp. 23-24, 44-52.

163. See Helfont, pp. 25-41, for a discussion of the Middle East regional implications of the three-way power struggle between Wahhabism, the Muslim Brotherhood, and Iran.

164. For Helfont's policy recommendations, see pp. 53-73. Helfont believes that it is imperative that the United States support neither Wahhabist nor Muslim Brotherhood organizations. He advocates treating such organizations separately, while pursuing broad support for open, stable societies throughout the region.

165. Studies of "those who support" radical Islam or terrorism are also called "demand side studies." The paucity of such studies is due in part to the size of the religion of Islam, the dangers in areas of conflict, and the requirement for significant resourcing. Also, there is the challenge of dividing radical Islam as religion from terrorism as tactic. Additionally, there are the terminological difficulties with unclear and overlapping meanings of the rule of *Shari'ah*, extremism, radicalism, *jihadism*, and Islamism, to name but a few. Finally, and perhaps most significantly, I believe there is the fear that demand side investigation might come off as judgmental.

166. See John L. Esposito and Dalia Mogahed, *Who Speaks for Islam?: What a Billion Muslims Really Think*, New York: Gallup Press, 2007. Esposito and Mogahed's book is long on interpretation, but short on the Gallup data it seeks to represent. In fact, the book does not contain one table or chart of data. The study has been criticized as subjective and unscientific. For a critique of this study, see Hillel Fradkin of Middle East Strategy at Harvard, Weatherhead Center, available from *blogs.law.harvard.edu/mesh/2008/04/who_does_speak_for_islam/*. See also the critique of Martin Kramer, a fellow at the Washington Institute for Near East Policy, and at the Adelson Institute for Strategic Studies, Shalem Center, and at the Olin Institute for Strategic Studies, Harvard University, available from *sandbox.blog-city.com/ dr_esposito_and_the_seven_percent_solution.htm*.

167. For the first applicable Islamic demographics from the Pew Research Center, see the first major report of the Pew Global Attitudes Project, *What the World Thinks in 2002*, Pew Global Attitudes Project, December 4, 2002, available from *people-press.org/reports/pdf/165.pdf* (henceforth, 2002 Pew Report). The Pew Research Center has continued to release regular Islamic studies, with the latest release of data in 2007.

168. C. Christine Fair and Bryan Shepherd, "Who Supports Terrorism?: Evidence from Fourteen Muslim Countries," *Studies in Conflict & Terrorism*, Vol. 29, No. 1, 2006, pp. 51-74. Conclusions cited are found at p. 71. Fair and Shepherd are aware of the limitation of the original data having been collected before Operation IRAQI FREEDOM. They wonder if the rates of support for terrorism would have been higher, had the data been collected later, see p. 73.

169. See *Support for Terror Wanes Among Muslim Publics*, Pew Global Attitudes Project, July 14, 2005, available from *pewglobal.org/reports/pdf/248.pdf* (henceforth, 2005 Pew Report). Also see *Muslim Americans: Middle Class and Mostly Mainstream*, Pew Research Center, May 22, 2007, available from *pewresearch.org/assets/pdf/muslim-americans.pdf*. (Henceforth, 2007 Pew Study.) This document also provides important data based on an April 2006 Pew Research Center survey of Muslims living in Muslim countries.

170. The 2005 Pew Report and the 2007 Pew Study both used the words "Islamic extremism" in its survey questions. The surveys themselves show the difficulty of using this nomenclature. My judgment is that the 2005 Pew Report and the 2007 Pew Study intend by this nomenclature to include all positions that would advocate any of the following: the rule of Shari'ah law at the governmental level, the potential legitimacy of violent *jihad*, and the potential legitimacy of the use of the tactics of terror. This would include all traditionalist positions—radical, conservative, and neotraditionalist—as well as terrorists. See related discussion at Tables 5 and 6.

171. The 2002 and 2005 Pew Reports, and the 2007 Pew Study, all fail to distinguish between acts which are part of militant *jihad*, which lies within the position of traditionalist Islam, and acts of terrorism. Also problematic is the pertinent survey question, which speaks of "suicide bombing and other forms of violence against civilians," failing to recognize terrorism which might be committed against service members. For example, acts of violence committed against wounded service members out of the fight, or against prisoners of war, or against service members of neutral forces participating in humanitarian relief operations, would be terrorist acts, judged according to the Geneva Conventions and the just war tradition. These limitations notwithstanding, the survey question helps shed light on how many Muslims would support terrorist acts as defined by Pew. See related discussion at Tables 7, 8, and 9.

172. See 2005 Pew Report, p. 34, for question "MQ.18" and responses. A number of respondents volunteered that they were equally Muslims and citizens.

173. *Ibid.*, pp. 34-35, for question "MQ.19" and responses. The 2002 data, drawn from the 2002 Pew Report and included at "MQ.19" of the 2005 Pew Report, does not appear to yield any remarkable conclusion.

174. See 2005 Pew Report, p. 35, for question "MQ.20" and responses.

175. See *ibid.*, p. 36, for question "MQ.25" and responses. The large numbers of those who could not or would not answer may suggest the possible inadequacy of the terminology "Muslim extremism."

176. See *ibid.*, pp. 36-37, for question "MQ.26" and responses.

177. This is question "QH.1" of the 2007 Pew Study, p. 91.

178. There is a somewhat hopeful trend demonstrated among those countries which were surveyed also in the earlier 2002, 2004, and 2005 Pew Reports. The 2007 Pew Study shows in Pakistan, Jordan, and Indonesia a decline among the rates of Muslims who find acts of terror justified; however, in Turkey there is an increase. All told, the overall rates remain high.

179. On the Muslim population of the United States, see 2007 Pew Study, p. 3. On the age breakdown of Muslims in the United States, Great Britain, France, Germany, and Spain relative to their support for suicide bombing and other terrorist acts, see 2007 Pew Study, p. 54. It is distressing that a reported 26 percent of Muslims in America ages 18-29 hold that such terrorist acts can be justified.

180. See 2005 Pew Report, 38, for question "MQ.31" and responses.

181. See Richard L. Pace, *The Role of Religion in the Life and Presidency of George W. Bush*, Strategic Research Project, Carlisle, PA: U.S. Army War College, March 19, 2004. See also Stephen Mansfield, *The Faith*

of George W. Bush, New York: J. P. Tarcher, 2003. Mansfield recounts that most United States Presidents have used religious language in their speeches, but notes, "By the early decades of the twentieth century, however, religion had declined as an influence in the United States, but presidents still spoke religiously of the nation as a nod to a Christian memory and as an attempt to baptize the American culture of their day," p. xvii.

182. See Pace, p. 8. Pace finds that certain of the terms President Bush used in connection with the Global War on Terrorism reflected "the lens of his personal faith." He cites examples such as "the axis of evil" and, regarding the war against terrorists, "Freedom and fear, justice and cruelty have always been at war, and we know that God is not neutral between them."

183. See Bob Woodward, *Bush at War*, New York: Simon & Schuster, 2002, p. 131. Woodward quotes President Bush's comments on the repressiveness of North Korea and Iraq:

> There is a human condition that we must worry about in times of war. There is a value system that cannot be compromised—God-given values. There aren't United States-created values. There are values of freedom and the human condition and mothers loving their children. What's very important as we articulate foreign policy through our diplomacy and military action, is that it never looks like we are creating—we are the author of these values."

184. Pace notes that President Bush used policy to support freedom of religion for *all* religions, because he viewed religious practice as one of the most basic universal freedoms; see p. 7. Had President Bush's policy been based on his own particular faith, it likely would not have supported freedom of religion for all faiths.

185. *The National Security Strategy of the United States of America*, September 17, 2002, available from *georgewbush-whitehouse.archives.gov/nsc/nss/2002/nss.pdf*; *The National Security Strategy of the United States of America*, March 16, 2006, available from *georgewbush-whitehouse.archives.gov/nsc/nss/2006/nss2006.pdf*.

186. NSS 2002, pp. iv, vi. Note that at p. vi, freedom is defined as the demand of human dignity; throughout the NSS freedom and human dignity are held to be two sides of the same coin. On the freedom as a universal value, see also p. 3: "The United States must defend liberty and justice because these principles are right and true for all people everywhere."

187. *Ibid.*, p. 3. The entire quote runs as follows: "America must stand firmly for the nonnegotiable demands of human dignity: the rule of law; limits on the absolute power of the state; free speech; freedom of worship; equal justice; respect for women; religious and ethnic tolerance; and respect for private property."

188. *Ibid.*, p. 4. The NSS 2002, did not limit to Muslim countries its promotion of religious freedom. In its discussion of the main centers of global power, the NSS 2002 argued that "only by allowing the Chinese people to think, assemble, and *worship freely* can China reach its full potential," p. 28, my emphasis.

189. *Ibid.*, p. 6: "We will also wage a war of ideas to win the battle against international terrorism. This includes: . . . supporting moderate and modern government, especially in the Muslim world, to ensure that the conditions and ideologies that promote terrorism do not find fertile ground in any nation."

190. NSS 2006, p. 7.

191. *Ibid.*, pp. 6-7.

192. *Ibid.*, p. 10.

193. *Ibid.*, p. 9.

194. The articulated long-term solution was to build democratic societies defined by ownership stake in society, the rule of law, freedom of speech, and the respect for human dignity; *ibid.*, pp. 10-11. The short-term solution was to prevent attacks by terrorist networks before they could occur, deny weapons of mass destruction to rogue states and terrorist allies, deny terrorist groups the support and sanctuary of rogue states, and deny terrorists the control of any nation that they could use as a base of operations; *ibid.*, p. 12.

195. President Obama's remarks at the National Prayer Breakfast, Washington, DC, February 5, 2009, available from *www.whitehouse.gov/blog_post/this_is_my_prayer/*.

196. *Ibid.* Within his prayer breakfast remarks, President Obama commented that his father was a Muslim who became an atheist, his grandparents were nonpracticing Methodists and Baptists, and his mother was skeptical of organized religion.

197. *Ibid.*

198. *Ibid.* The pertinent text reads in full:

We know too that whatever our differences, there is one law that binds all great religions together. Jesus told us to "love thy neighbor as thyself." The Torah commands, "That which is hateful to you, do not do to your fellow." In Islam, there is a hadith that reads "None of you truly believes until he wishes for his brother what he wishes for himself." And the same is true for Buddhists and Hindus; for followers of Confucius and for humanists. It is, of course, the Golden Rule—the call to love one another; to understand one another; to treat with dignity and respect those with whom we share a brief moment on this Earth.

Many adherents of these, and other, world religions would argue that the moral imperatives of their faiths are not the same. That said, western theological liberalism frequently interprets the religions of the world as cut from the same cloth.

199. *Ibid.*

200. As of the writing of this manuscript, President Obama had published no National Security Strategy. To access the speeches of President Obama which I have used as sources, see President Obama's Inaugural Address, Washington, DC, January 20, 2009, available from *www. whitehouse.gov/the_press_office/ President_Barack_Obamas_Inaugural_ Address*. President Obama's remarks to the Turkish Parliament, Ankara, Turkey, April 6, 2009, available from *www.whitehouse.gov/the_press_office/Remarks-By-President-Obama-To-The-Turkish-Parliament/*. President Obama's "On a New Beginning" speech at Cairo University, Cairo, Egypt, June 4, 2009, available from *www.whitehouse.gov/the_press_office/Remarks-by-the-President-at-Cairo-University-6-04-09/*. President Obama's "New Moment of Promise" speech to the Ghanaian Parliament in Accra, Ghana, July 11, 2009, available from *www.whitehouse.gov/the_press_office/Remarks-by-the-President-to-the-Ghanaian-Parliament/*. President Obama's remarks at the memorial service at Fort Hood and III Corps, Fort Hood, TX, November 10, 2009, available from *www.whitehouse.gov/the-press-office/remarks-president-memorial-service-fort-hood*. President Obama's "On the Way Forward in Afghanistan and Pakistan" speech at West Point, NY, December 1, 2009, available from *www.whitehouse.gov/the-press-office/remarks-president-address-nation-way-forward-afghanistan-and-pakistan*.

201. From Ankara, the following quote is representative of President Obama's speech:

The United States is not, and will never be, at war with Islam. In fact, our partnership with the Muslim world is critical not just in rolling back the violent ideologies that people of all faiths reject, but also to strengthen opportunity for all its people.

I also want to be clear that America's relationship with the Muslim community, the Muslim world, cannot, and will not, just be based upon opposition to terrorism. We seek broader engagement based on mutual interest and mutual respect. We will listen carefully, we will bridge misunder-standings, and we will seek common ground. We will be respectful, even when we do not agree. We will convey our deep appreciation for the Islamic faith, which has done so much over the centuries to shape the world—including in my own country.

202. From Ankara, while speaking about his support for Turkey's bid to join the European Union (EU), President Obama commented that the EU would stand to gain by the "diversity of ethnicity, tradition and faith" that Turkey would bring. He then proceeded to encourage Turkey in its reforms, for "freedom of religion and expression lead to a strong and vibrant civil society."

203. From Cairo, regarding terrorists: "Their actions are irreconcilable with the rights of human beings, the progress of nations, and with Islam."

204. From Cairo, the full quote runs as follows:

There's one rule that lies at the heart of every religion—that we do unto others as we would have them do unto us. This truth transcends nations and peoples—a belief that isn't new; that isn't black or white or brown; that isn't Christian or Muslim or Jew. It's a belief that pulsed in the cradle of civilization, and that still beats in the hearts of billions around the world. It's a faith in other people, and it's what brought me here today.

We have the power to make the world we seek, but only if we have the courage to make a new beginning.

205. From Accra, the full quote runs as follows: "Defining oneself in opposition to someone who belongs to a different tribe, or who worships a different prophet, has no place in the 21st century. Africa's diversity should be a source of strength, not a cause for division. We are all God's children."

206. On November 10, 2009, President Obama spoke at a memorial service at Fort Hood, TX, in the wake of the November 5, 2009, terrorist attack. As of the writing of this manuscript, Major Nidal Malik Hasan stands accused of opening fire and killing 13, and wounding 30 others, while shouting *Allahu Akbar*, "God is great" in Arabic. All but one of the casualties were soldiers. These casualty figures are from the official U.S. Army Home Page. Other authorities cite 14 dead, including the unborn infant of one slain pregnant soldier, and 38 wounded. See C. Todd Lopez, "President Says Nation Will Always Remember Fort Hood Casualties," November 11, 2009, at *The United States Army Home Page*, available from *www.army.mil/-news/2009/11/11/30179-president-says-nation-will-always-remember-fort-hood-casualties/index.html*.

207. From West Point, the full quote runs as follows:

We'll have to use diplomacy, because no one nation can meet the challenges of an interconnected world acting alone. I've spent this year renewing our alliances and forging new partnerships. And we have forged a new beginning between America and the Muslim world—one that recognizes our mutual interest in breaking a cycle of conflict, and that promises a future in which those who kill innocents are isolated by those who stand up for peace and prosperity and human dignity.

208. Here I am leaving aside the added strategic message in the NSS 2006, which characterized Islam as a proud religion being twisted by terrorists for evil purposes. Because President Obama has taken this message and more fully developed it, I provide analysis in my discussion of the paradigm suggested by President Obama's policy—the paradigm of Religion as Unity.

209. I am not intending to convey a comprehensive plan that uses all elements of national power to the defeat the adversary, but only a sketch of some of the policy implications of the paradigm of Religion as Freedom.

210. On the decisive question of how Islam is to achieve its universalization, and the answers of various positions, see the discussion beginning on p.16 above.

211. On alignments within traditionalist Islam, see pp. 20-22 above.

212. Here I am leaving aside the additional note sounded in President Obama's speeches at Ankara and Cairo, in which he encouraged diversity of religious expression for building strong and vibrant societies. Because President Bush more fully developed this thought, I provide analysis in my discussion of the paradigm suggested by President Bush's policy—the paradigm of Religion as Freedom.

213. On the varying faith positions within Islam, see Table 1. On demographics which show the level of Muslim support for ever justifying terrorist acts, see Table 8.

214. On the decisive question of how Islam is to achieve its universalization, and the answers of various positions, see the discussion beginning on p. 16 above.

215. The pertinent portion of the First Amendment to the U.S. Constitution reads, "Congress shall make no law respecting an establishment of religion, or prohibiting the free exercise thereof."

216. I am indebted to Chaplain (Colonel) Micheal Hoyt of the Office of the Army Chief of Chaplains, DACH-3/5/7, for his analysis regarding options for strengthening religion within campaign planning.

APPENDIX

GLOSSARY OF KEY ISLAMIC TERMS

dar al-harb – the territory of war.

dar al-Islam – the territory of Islam.

dhimmitude – the second class citizenship status of Jews and Christians within lands conquered by Islam.

fatwa – a formal restatement, or new application, of Islamic law.

fitnah - sedition or idolatry.

hadith – customary law written down by Mohammed's Companions.

iman – the true faith.

jihad - struggle (varying interpretations of application.)

mujahideen – Muslim warriors.

naskh – abrogation. A principle of interpretation which allows certain later passages of the *Qur'an* and elements of *Shari'ah* to take precedence over earlier passages or elements.

Qur'an - documentation of a series of revelations to the Prophet Mohammed; the primary authority for Islam.

Shari'ah – the law in Islam that effects the rule of God and governs life – individual, community, and state.

sirah - biographical accounts of Mohammed's life.

siyar – the Islamic law of nations (includes the Islamic law of war).

Sunnah - the second authority in Islam, composed of the words, deeds, and judgments of Mohammad, to include community practice flowing from the Prophet's example.

surah – a chapter in the Qur'an.

ummah - the one community of Islamic believers worldwide.

usul al-fiqh – principles of Islamic jurisprudence.